Malt Whisky

A Comprehensive Guide for
both Novice and Connoisseur

Malt Whisky

A Comprehensive Guide for
both Novice and Connoisseur

Graham Nown

PUBLISHED BY
SALAMANDER BOOKS LIMITED
LONDON

A Salamander Book

Published by Salamander Books Ltd
129–137 York Way
London N7 9LG
United Kingdom

This edition distributed by
SMITHMARK Publishers,
a division of U.S. Media Holdings, Inc.,
115 West 18th Street,
New York, NY 10011.

9 8 7 6 5 4 3 2 1

SMITHMARK books are available for bulk purchase for sales promotion and premium use. For details write or call the manager of special sales, SMITHMARK Publishers, 115 West 18th Street, New York, NY 10011; (212) 532-6600.

ISBN 0-7651-9362-0

Printed in Italy

All correspondence concerning the content of this volume should be addressed to Salamander Books Ltd.

Credits

Editor: Alice Duke
Designer: Paul Johnson
Map illustrations: Kathy Baxendale
Color separation: PixelTech Pte, Singapore
Filmset: SX DTP

Contents

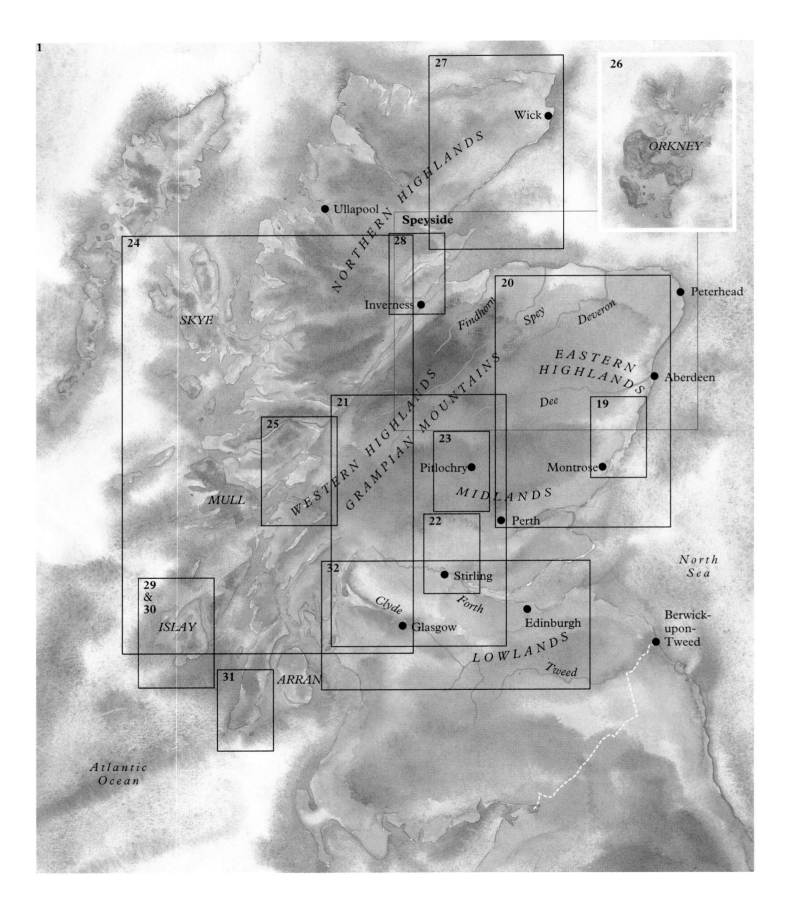

1

27

Wick ●

26

ORKNEY

● Ullapool

NORTHERN HIGHLANDS

Speyside

24

28

Inverness ●

SKYE

Findhorn   Spey   Deveron

20

Peterhead ●

EASTERN
HIGHLANDS

Aberdeen ●

Dee

19

21

25

WESTERN HIGHLANDS

GRAMPIAN MOUNTAINS

23

Pitlochry ●

MIDLANDS

Montrose ●

MULL

22

Perth ●

32

Stirling ●

North
Sea

29
&
30

Clyde

Forth

ISLAY

Glasgow ●

Edinburgh ●

Berwick-
upon-
Tweed ●

31

ARRAN

LOWLANDS

Tweed

Atlantic
Ocean

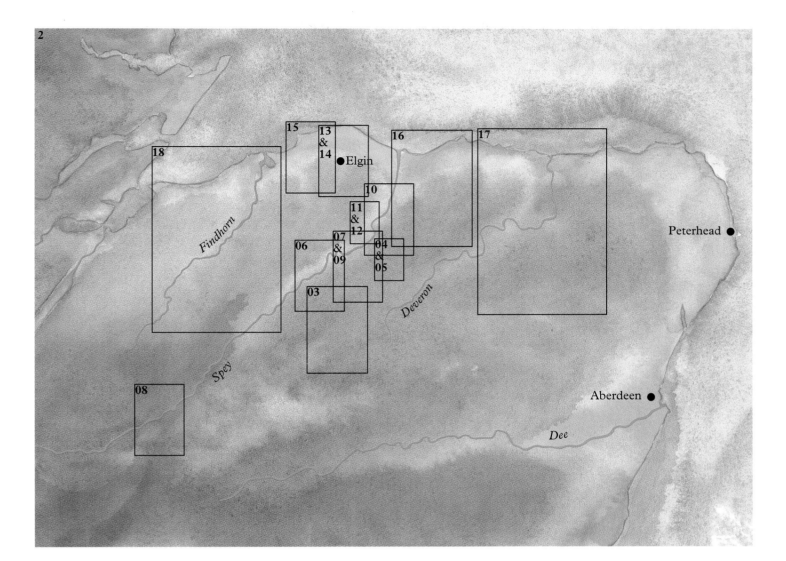

Nature's Gift

*"It remains a mystery when the art of distilling first reached Britain.
What is certain is that the ancient Celts practised the art and had an expressive name
for the fiery liquid they produced – uisge beatha – 'the water of life'."*

Scotch Whisky Association

Anyone who has visited Scotland or toured a distillery cannot fail to notice that most single malt whisky is produced in the remotest locations of the Highlands and Islands. Whisky making began as part of the seasonal cycle of farming life and even in the nineteenth century, was still a cottage industry. Many of today's distilleries occupy the sites of original farms and some maintain the link by keeping them in operation.

The story of how whisky developed into one of Britain's biggest earners is a tribute to Scots tenacity: a determination to distil their national spirit and ensure its survival through oppression, excessive taxation and economic hardship.

Natural ingredients

Single malt Scotch whisky – distilled from malted barley at a single Scottish distillery and matured for not less than three years – uses only natural ingredients: water, peat and barley.

The first distilleries were built in areas where these ingredients were found in abundance.

Scotland has the perfect cool, damp conditions for making and maturing whisky. Despite winter gales and blizzards, overall temperatures are quite moderate. Even the language Highlanders use to describe the weather is temperate: it's never cold, always "fresh"; it seldom rains, but there's an abundance of "Scotch mist".

Barley grows particularly well in Scottish latitudes, especially in the sheltered plains of the Black Isle, close to where Speyside whiskies are produced, while peat is a universal commodity, covering the Highlands in a thick mantle laid down over thousands of years. Rights to cut peat for fuel are still exercized today. On Islay, for example, any islander can cut and dry his own supplies for just £13 a year.

Pure stream water from springs, rainfall or "snow-bree", as

the Scots term melted snow, criss-cross the country, collecting minerals and trace elements as they run through peat, over granite and down to distilleries.

Given this abundant wealth around them, it is no surprise the Scots regarded the ingredients for making whisky as a gift from nature and resented attempts to tax or control it.

Seasonal cycle

Centuries ago whisky was made from October to May, immediately after the late September barley harvest, in the cool months when yeast is less volatile and easy to control. Protein-rich by-products of the distilling process were used – indeed still are – as winter cattle feed in the months when grass contained little nourishment.

Whisky slotted into the natural cycle, a way of using excess grain to make a product which could be sold, bartered or taken as a medicine for colic, palsy, smallpox and a list of other ailments. The distilling of whisky, as someone put it, made a harsh existence bearable.

Whisky: a way of life

Irrespective of what a Scot wears under his kilt, there is no mystery about what he carried in his sporran: "chuckies", balls of whisky-soaked oats to keep the cold at bay on long, cross-country journeys.

Until the nineteenth century, Scotch whisky was not matured, but often run straight from the still into jugs and jars. To cool its fiery qualities and remove the raw edge from the new spirit, herbs and spices were added to make young whisky palatable. Unsurprisingly, this volcanic concoction remained too robust and challenging for delicate English palates. Without the smoothness maturation afforded, early malt whisky was strictly an acquired taste and, in the case of many Highlanders, one they acquired in their mothers' arms – toddlers were commonly offered a fortifying tot.

From cradle to grave, whisky was an intrinsic part of Scottish life. It is still used to greet a guest, "wet the baby's head", toast the bride and groom and provide an appropriate send-off for the departed.

Mysterious origins

No one is quite sure when distilling came to Scotland. The art was probably developed in the Middle East, where Alexandrines

Left: Scottish barley ripe for harvesting – the goodness packed into its short growing season makes it ideal for whisky production.

Above: Eduard Grissner's Monks in their Beer Cellar. *Monks displaced by the dissolution of the monasteries turned their talents to distilling.*

were distilling in AD 900. The word "alcohol" comes from the Arabic and the secrets of condensing vapors from a copper pot were studied by alchemists in medieval Europe.

The interior of some of today's distilleries may resemble the control room of a power station, but there remains, nevertheless, a strong sense of the mysterious elements of fire, earth, air and water at work.

The general belief is that the art wound its way from the East, through Europe, to Ireland, where monks adept at brewing ale perfected it. At least half the whisky-making process, as we shall see, differs only slightly from that of making beer.

St. Patrick is often credited with carrying the knowledge to Scotland, though there is no evidence to support this. The Scots, who gave the country its name, originally came from Ireland, several centuries after the Picts.

If pot distilling followed this route, then Islay, less than twenty-five miles (40km) away, and Campbeltown, on the Mull of Kintyre, a dozen miles (19km) from Antrim, may be the likeliest crucible of whisky making.

The water of life

What is sure is that Scotland was perfect for making whisky. The earliest evidence of distilling is a document from 1494 which records, "eight bolls of malt from Friar John Cor wherewith to make aquavitae".

The Latin *aquavitae*, the Gaelic *uisge beatha* or the French *eau de vie*, all translated as "the water of life". A boll, originally a Scandinavian measure, was equal to about thirty-five pounds (16kg), which was enough malt to make at least 1,500 bottles of whisky.

We can assume that this was no early tentative experiment. Distilling had been around in Scotland at least since the Middle Ages, probably much earlier – spores found by archaeologists on the Isle of Rhum in 1986 indicate that "an alcoholic drink" may have been made there 6,000 years ago. In the sixteenth and seventeenth centuries whisky making was improved and developed by monks seeking useful outlets for their skills following the dissolution of the monasteries.

Today, regardless of modern refinements to improve quality and speed production, the way Scotch whisky is made has changed surprisingly little over the centuries.

The spirit of Scotland

Distilling took to the hills when duty was levied on whisky. Highlanders regarded it as an outrage that their way of life and freely available local ingredients were to be taxed to swell government coffers.

Aware of whisky's wide popularity, politicians saw distilling as an attractive source of revenue. The first of many excise duties was announced by the Scots parliament in 1644, when thirteen pence was imposed on a Scots pint (one third of a gallon) to raise money for Oliver Cromwell's civil war against Charles I's royalists.

Without exception, Highland whisky makers ignored the tax and, with a marked absence of roads in rural Scotland, there was little the authorities could do. However, undeterred by their singular lack of success, ever-increasing taxes and restrictions were heaped upon malt and its end-product, whisky.

The excise war

Highlanders who continued to disregard duty and defiantly distil in their glens were finally driven underground by the 1707 Act of Union, which brought England and Scotland together under one parliament. The political purpose of the Act was a single economic and foreign policy, but a less publicized aim was to control rebellious Scottish clans and "civilize" the Highlands.

One early move was to establish a more effective Excise Board. Soon, additional excisemen or "gaugers" poured across the border and became a common sight in Scotland. Worse was to come. In the aftermath of 1715, when the Jacobite uprising in support of a Scottish monarchy was crushed, new roads were laid across the country by General Wade to control increasingly troublesome Highlanders. Illicit distillers, now within easier reach of the authorities, had to go to ground to avoid detection.

Mountains and remote glens were crossed by caravans of hardy ponies laden with kegs of illicit whisky to barter for goods. Whisky trails with names like "the ladder", "Jock's road" and "the fungle" were unmarked on maps and largely unknown to the authorities.

Outwitting the gaugers

The next hundred years became a monument to Scottish ingenuity as smugglers sought to evade gaugers and transport their whisky to expanding markets in England.

Below: Scotland's rugged terrain not only provided the natural ingredients for making whisky, but also the perfect cover for smugglers.

Right: Whisky drinkers in 1840. Scotch whisky, more than any other spirit, has been widely celebrated in poetry and song.

In 1823, when legal whisky making was encouraged, one of the first distillers to take out a licence was George Smith, who founded Glenlivet distillery.

One illicit distiller funnelled smoke underground from his hidden still to a cottage seventy yards (64m) away, where it emerged innocently from the chimney. On more than one occasion whisky was carried by coffin on the shoulders of "mourners" past vigilant excisemen, or stored beneath the pulpits of Church of Scotland ministers .

Meanwhile, those magistrates who as landowners supplied distillers with barley were understandably lenient when cases were brought before their courts. As one Campbeltown woman protested to the sheriff when she was arrested, "I have nae made a drop since that wee keg I sent you".

Spirit of independence
After the defeat of Scots loyal to Bonnie Prince Charlie at Culloden in 1746, the government ruthlessly suppressed all symbols of patriotism: tartan and wearing kilts were banned, along with playing the bagpipes. The handful of distilleries struggling to make legitimate whisky were almost wiped out by another heavy increase in duty.

> To incite Scots to spy on each other, £5 was offered to anyone reporting illicit distilling equipment. Canny smugglers handed in their worn out copper coils, or "worms", used to condense spirit vapors. The reward was spent on refurbishing their stills.

Outside the law, whisky production in the Highlands and Islands continued unabated. "Freedom an' whisky gang thegither!", as Robert Burns aptly noted in "The Author's Earnest Cry And Prayer".

Across the border, England, in the grip of a "gin epidemic", was facing drink problems of its own. In fact, public drunkenness became such a problem that in 1750 the Gin Act was passed to restore order. Scots grabbed this opportunity to sell their whisky in England and, despite every effort by the authorities to curtail illicit distilling, smuggling was stepped up.

Between 1793 and 1803 tax on whisky climbed crazily from £9 to an incredible £162 in a ten-year period. The result was that more Scots than ever turned to illegal distilling to pay their rent.

As the nineteenth century dawned, one effect of harsh legislation was to divide Scotch whisky into two distinct types, Highland and Lowland. Because of crippling duties, legitimate Lowland distillers were forced to produce poorer whisky, with less malt and more duty-free raw grain, to stay in business. Highland whisky, made cheaply from an abundance of natural ingredients, became regarded as authentic single malt. It was certainly skilfully manufactured, often by reputable distillers who had taken to the hills after being bankrupted by duties.

The approach of peace
Profit was not always the prime consideration in whisky making. Scots regarded distilling their national spirit as an act of patriotism. Illicit stills thrived even in cities where risk of detection ran high. At one time, Edinburgh, for example, had eight licensed and 400 unlicensed stills.

By the early 1800s, when Speyside boasted almost 4,000 illicit stills and not one legal one, even the government began to realize how impossible the situation had become. More than 14,000 raids were carried out in 1820 by excisemen who reported that collecting revenue was an unending struggle.

Finally, an olive branch was offered in the shape of a highly stage-managed visit to Scotland by George IV in 1822. To the amusement of Edinburgh crowds, the portly monarch wore a kilt and publicly took a glass of Glenlivet at a dinner.

Reconciliation enabled the Duke of Gordon, one of Scotland's biggest landowners, to smooth the way for new legislation the following year. For a modest fee of £10 anyone could take out a licence to legally operate a still of more than forty gallons (182 litres/48 US gallons).

One by one, whisky distillers came in from the cold. Farms developed into distilleries as demand for legal whisky grew. Scotch began to take its first steps on the road to becoming an international spirit.

The birth of blending

The only whiskies the English found to their taste in the early 1800s were light, palatable Lowland malts, which lacked the bold individuality of Highland and Island spirits. South of the border, the upper classes preferred brandy, convinced that whisky had little to offer.

It took an Irishman – and an exciseman at that – to change their view, along with some accidental help from the French. In early Victorian times the only Scotch whisky was malt whisky. It was distilled, as today, from a fermented "beery" wash in a distinctively shaped copper still. Products of the first distillation were then distilled a second time.

It was laborious, time-consuming work, but the reward was a single malt whisky with an individual character borrowed from its locality.

Welcome to grain whisky

In 1830 Aeneas Coffey, a former excise inspector who worked at Dublin's Dock Distillery, turned tradition on its head. He became fascinated by an ingenious still invented a few years earlier by a renowned Scots whisky maker, Robert Stein. It was a continuous process which could work around the clock distilling alcohol cheaply from any kind of grain, including maize, rye and oats.

Coffey's improved version consisted of two tall adjoining towers called an analyzer and a rectifier. The idea was simple: fermented wash, similar to ale, entered the top of the first tower and fell to meet scalding steam rising from the base. When the two collided on layers of perforated plates, the wash boiled, alcohol vaporized and ascended to the top of the column. It was then pumped into the base of the adjoining tower, or rectifier, and condensed on a long metal coil.

Grain versus malt

Grain whisky was bland and light in body and aroma. In the eyes of some distillers it had several advantages over single malt. The process was fast and relatively inexpensive. Grain spirit also came off the still at higher strength than the pot still process: 94.8 per cent against single malt which is drawn off between 64 per cent and 74 per cent, depending on the stillman's preference.

Grain spirit wasn't new. It had been made in pot stills since the seventeeth century from wheat and maize, which were cheaper than malted barley. The difference was that Coffey's continuous still could be located anywhere. Unlike single malts, which were tied to supplies of water, peat and malted barley, Coffey stills could be built in the heart of Lowland cities, with good rail and road connections.

> Blended whisky is designed to appeal to the widest possible international market and please as many drinkers as possible. Single malts – the château wines of the whisky world – are uniquely individual and admired for their quirks of character.

One continuous still could produce more in a week than a single malt distillery's output for a whole year. Today the output of Scotland's six grain distilleries exceeds that of its ninety or so malt distilleries combined.

The mid-nineteenth century was also the age in which the benefits of maturation – the chemical changes that round whisky's rough edges when it rests in wood – were rapidly being discovered. Because of its composition, grain whisky matured faster than malt and was therefore ready for sale earlier.

The perfect partnership

The first substantial breakthrough in Scotch whisky sales came in the 1860s when the Edinburgh firm of Andrew Usher

THE INDISPENSABLE USHER.

THE "USHER" INDISPENSABLE AT EVERY FUNCTION SINCE THE DAYS OF
GEORGE THE THIRD, IS USHER'S WHISKY.

Obtainable through all Wine Merchants and Stores in the United Kingdom.

ANDREW USHER & CO., Distillers, EDINBURGH.   London and Export Agents: FRANK BAILEY & CO., 30, MARK LANE, E.C.

began blending malt and grain whiskies into a smooth, palatable whisky suited to English tastes.

No one knows the recipe used in the first blended whisky, Usher's Old Vatted Glenlivet, though it was probably neither very old, nor had a high Glenlivet content. Nevertheless, it was an historic moment, opening the door to new markets.

The timing couldn't have been better. A few years earlier, in 1858, the English market had been opened wide when disaster struck French vineyards, bankrupting brandy manufacturers. A burrowing aphid, *Phylloxera vastatrix*, found its way from Californian vineyards to France. It was less harmful to American-grown vines, but wiped out French vineyards by feeding on the roots of the plant. For the next eight years French wine producers grafted their own varieties onto American root stocks. (A legacy of this is that modern vines do not live as long as they did previously.)

Whisky's society debut

London clubs and restaurants, the heartland of brandy and soda, ran dry and in desperation turned to whisky as an alternative. Whisky barons like Tom Dewar and James Buchanan, and many others, descended on London in a determined crusade to convert the upper classes in the knowledge that if they succeeded the middle and working classes would eventually follow. They courted influence in high places, signed cheques to swell political funds in exchange for promises, stabbed each other in the back and laid the foundations for lucrative long-term deals.

By the time the French wine industry had recovered, and brandy stocks were replenished, it was too late; Scotch whisky had seized the high ground. Whisky and soda became Sherlock Holmes' favorite drink; Dickens, too, developed a taste for Scotch – when he died, thirty-four cases of Highland malt from Cockburns of Leith were found in his cellar. Whisky's pioneering entrepreneurs changed the drinking habits of a country, and having achieved that, they set their sights on overseas sales.

Making a masterpiece

Today's blends are a far cry from the original Usher's Old Vatted Glenlivet. Anything from fifteen to fifty single malts may be combined with grain whiskies to give them their own distinctive character. Each component whisky enhances the flavor of the whole, rather like the instruments of an orchestra. Allied Distillers master blender Robert Hicks compares his art to painting a masterpiece in oils. "Grain is the foundation, the way we prepare the canvas," he says. "If you do not prime the canvas properly with several coats of bland, pale colors, it will not hold the oils or show them to their best advantage. An artist sketches the outline of his picture in charcoal. I use Highland whiskies to create the broad outline of the style I am looking for. Later, the colors are filled in with the Speysides, the Islays and the Islands."

When the blender has selected his whiskies, they are brought from the warehouse, mixed in a vat and left to "marry" in casks for a few months before bottling. Some prefer to vat their malts and grains separately, bringing them together just before bottling. The exact proportions are usually a closely guarded secret.

Which blend?

If a blended bottle carries an age statement, it refers to the age of the youngest whisky in the blend. A blend classified as "de luxe" or "premium" is older, 10 Years Old or more, and would be expected to have up to 60 per cent malt whisky in it. "Super de luxe" blends are usually not less than 20 Years Old and should contain around 75 per cent malt.

The wonderful thing about whisky is that it is a personal experience. The choice of malts in an expensive blend may not suit the palate of one drinker as much as a perfectly good cheaper blend. However, usually, the greater the number of malts, the more interesting and sophisticated the whisky.

For many years, in some cases until the 1960s, many single malt distilleries did not bottle their whisky for the public, but sold it almost entirely within the trade for blending. It was left to grocers and specialist merchants to buy casks and bottle individual malts for general sale.

The rise in popularity of single malt Scotch whisky, with its intriguing shades and complexities, is a comparatively recent phenomenon, and long overdue.

Left: A promotion for Usher's blended whisky. Whisky seized the high ground when brandy imports were hit by a plague in French vineyards.

Below: A Punch *cartoon of 1876 by Charles Keene shows whisky's increasing acceptance in fashionable English Society.*

Modern times

In the twentieth century, the final chapter in the story of Scotch whisky is a mixture of set back and success. Its rise to become a star performer on the world spirits stage has not been achieved without a struggle.

The new century dawned with an unexpected court case, brought by zealous trading standards officers in the London borough of Islington. Before long this 1905 local dispute escalated into a heated debate, culminating in a Royal Commission to define exactly which spirit was worthy of the appellation "authentic Scotch". Was it single malt, grain whisky, or blended whisky, the hybrid of both?

The action was triggered by the sale of poor spirits passed off as brandy in the wake of the phylloxera epidemic. Several London councils hauled publicans before the courts under the Food and Drugs Act for selling inferior produce. Spurred on by their success, Islington council officers turned their attention to whisky. They swooped on local pubs and retailers, analyzing brands and serving summonses.

Four hundred miles (644km) away in Scotland, the prosecutions opened an old wound. Despite an economic slump in the wake of the Boer War, whisky blenders were enjoying an era of unprecedented wealth from sales south of the border.

Distillers of single malts, or "selfs", had long been irritated by the popularity and earning power of grain whisky at the expense of their characterful spirits. To make matters worse, blended whisky was advertised everywhere as "Scotch whisky", when they believed their own product was the only genuine article.

The "what is whisky?" case

By the time the case reached Islington Magistrates' Court in London, grain and malt distillers had dug in for a major battle. The magistrate ruled against local publicans who had been selling blended whisky as "Scotch". Furious grain distillers and blenders financed an appeal.

A board of seven magistrates failed to reach a decision and malt distillers claimed victory. The case attracted great publicity and the grain lobby, fearful of jeopardizing future sales, pressured the Board of Trade to appoint a Royal Commission.

Malt distillers testified that, according to tradition, Scotch whisky could only be made from malted barley, pot-distilled and matured in Scotland. Grain supporters claimed that blended whisky was not only made in Scotland, but also contained fewer impurities and improved with ageing, just like single malt whisky.

The Royal Commission verdict, published in 1909 after thirty-seven sittings and evidence from 116 witnesses, ruled

that both could rightfully call themselves Scotch whisky. Henceforth, the definition of Scotch became "a spirit obtained by distillation from a mash of cereal grain [this now meant barley or other grains, such as wheat or corn], 'saccharified' by the diastase of malt [converted to soluble sugars by malt enzymes]." And, of course, distilled in Scotland.

The official definition of whisky

This first legal definition established Scotch whisky as a unique product with a singular identity and discouraged imitators. Six years later there was further fine tuning: single malt, grain or blended spirits had to mature for three years in wood before they could be called whisky.

In 1988 the Scotch Whisky Act went further to ensure that whisky remains a natural product: taste and aroma may come only from its raw materials; distillation and maturation must also take place in Scotland.

The big thirst

Scotch whisky was well on the way to becoming a popular international drink, but a set back came at the end of the First World War, when the United States, a lucrative market, declared Prohibition. At midnight on 16 January 1920 saloons closed throughout the nation. As the temperance lobby celebrated removing alcohol from the population's reach, "the

The value of all Scotch whisky exports in 1995 was £2,276 million. The lion's share (42 per cent) went to Europe, while other key consumers were the USA (13 per cent), Latin America (12 per cent) and Asia (12 per cent). Of the European exports, 19 per cent of bottled single malts were consumed in Britain, closely followed by 15 per cent in Italy and 14 per cent in France.

noble experiment" triggered an insatiable thirst. Scotland found itself unprepared. Of 153 distilleries open in 1905, war restrictions had reduced the working number to only eight. Lloyd George had tried to impose prohibition of his own to discourage drunkenness among munitions workers, but he had failed to win support and doubled excise duty instead. Distilleries, struggling with wartime grain shortages had closed or gone out of business.

Scotch whisky companies lost no time making deals with bootleggers, who would stop at nothing to beat the Customs blockade. In New York City some even purchased a redundant U-boat and fired bottles of whisky onto Long Island beaches inside torpedo heads.

Despite a reluctance among many police and customs officers to uphold the unpopular law, others enforced it zealously. Officers Izzy Einstein and Moe Smith, with a Laurel and Hardy approach and a penchant for disguises, raided 3,000 speakeasies, arrested 4,900 drinkers and confiscated five million bottles of spirit in the first five years of Prohibition.

The Scotch whisky industry rose to the challenge. To cope

Left: Liquor-laden torpedoes seized by customs aboard the schooner MB Rosie. *Each contained forty gallons (180 litres/48 US gallons of whisky.*

Below: The repeal of Prohibition brought relief to the whisky industry. Legal stocks quickly piled up at Southampton awaiting shipment.

In 1947 excise duty on a litre of Scotch was three pounds and sixty eight pence: today, half a century on, it is almost twenty pounds.

with demand, 130 distilleries were back in production by the 1920s. Irish whiskey, which once outsold Scotch in America, lost the initiative and never fully regained its impetus. In terms of world sales, Scotch still dominates.

But dark clouds gathered; the 1926 General Strike and economic depression brought a down-turn in whisky sales in Britain. When Prohibition was repealed in 1933, glasses had hardly been raised to John Barleycorn's return before another world war brought more rationing, grain shortages and further increases in duty to fund military spending.

The industry prospered in the post-war years, but over-production and the world recession of the mid-1980s created a "whisky loch", which heralded a depressing period of mergers, rationalization, cost-cutting and distillery closures.

Today there are around ninety working single malt distilleries in Scotland producing around 12,750,000 gallons (58 million litres/15,312,000 US gallons) annually. Public interest has never been higher and more bottlings than ever are available. Only excessive taxation prevents more enthusiasts raising a dram to celebrate malt whisky's welcome revival.

Singular Malt

"There's no such thing as bad whiskey.
Some whiskeys just happen to be better than others."

William Faulkner (1897–1962)

Many countries distil their own malt whisky, with varying degrees of success. National pride aside, little among "the slavish herd", as Horace called imitators, competes with the depth and complexity of Scottish single malts. What makes them so special? Ironically, the simple answer is found, not in Scotland, but overseas.

In places where they haven't yet learned better, a belief persists that anyone can make Scotch whisky. All you need is the same yeast and barley and a similar-shaped still. The fact that the original is distilled and matured in Scotland's unique environment seems neither here nor there.

The Swedes were among the first to explore the theory in 1939, when the Lowland distillery of Bladnoch – the most southerly in Scotland – lay padlocked, its workers having been called up for the war effort.

When the company responsible for this delightful, dry whisky was forced into liquidation, some enthusiastic Swedish prospectors swooped on the auction of distillery equipment, and Bladnoch's stills, which produced a delicate, grassy malt, were unceremoniously stripped and shipped to Scandinavia. However, legend has it that the experiment was not quite the success it was hoped. There is an unconfirmed story that when Bladnoch acquired new owners, the stills quietly found their way back to Scotland, making it, as one former manager wryly put it, "the only distillery to have been away on holiday".

The search goes on

More celebrated is the story of Alko, the Finnish state distilling company, which devoted ten years to divining the secrets of Scotch whisky.

A decade on, 800 compounds had been isolated in Finnish laboratories with no sign of a whisky to rival a Scottish single malt. Alko's head of research, Lalli Nykänen, (who has admitted a preference for 12 Years Old Glenlivet) estimated it might take another ten years to discover what makes the flavor.

Few efforts have been more determined than those of the Japanese to discover what sets Scottish malt apart. One Islay distillery manager, weary of a group of Japanese trade visitors photographing his stills, asked them to leave their cameras in his office. Later, he discovered one of the party sketching the equipment on the back of an envelope.

What sets scotch whisky apart?

The universal fascination with Scottish single malt whisky lies in its uniqueness and the way in which style and flavor are reflected by region. Single malts distil not only the essence of the country, its landscape and history, but convey a sense of the precise geographical location of each distillery.

If this sounds far-fetched, consider the neighboring Inverness distilleries of Glen Mhor (*glen vor*), sadly demolished, and Glen Albyn, now a supermarket, which used to face each other across the Great North Road before closing down in the slump of the 1980s. Both drew their water from Loch Ness and, though situated only yards apart, made entirely different whisky: Glen Albyn a pale, sweet relatively undistinguished whisky; Glen Mhor celebrated for its freshness, balance and full flavor.

A good single malt acquires its identity in several ways. Its smokey dryness is determined by how much peat smoke the barley is exposed to at the malting stage. The cereal itself contributes a general sweetness, but individual varieties do not have a decisive effect on flavor.

The wonder of water

Water, however, has a unique importance in determining a whisky's character. There are stories of distilleries drawing supplies from opposite sides of the same hill, yet making two quite different whiskies. The rocks over which a distillery's water supply tumbles and the quality of peat it cuts through, provide traces of minerals and vegetation which make vital contributions to the finished product.

"A source of good soft water is essential to a distillery," the Scotch Whisky Association says. However, to confuse the issue, Glenmorangie's celebrated water from Tarlogie Springs is hard, as are the "limey" burns used by Highland Park in Orkney and several Speyside distilleries.

There is an old belief that the best whisky water flows "through peat over granite", despite the fact (or perhaps because of it) that granite's tough, impervious nature allows few minerals to be extracted. A reliable view, put forward by the whisky expert, Michael Moss, is that soft, peaty water tends to produce good heavy malts, while harder water lends itself to lighter styles.

Laphroaig (*la-froyg*) distillery, home of one of Islay's pungent, smokey whiskies, spent decades locked in costly litigation with a rival over its precious water source. Ardenistiel was deliberately built next door to capitalize on its success. Yet, while Laphroaig remains one of the world's most strikingly individual whiskies, the pale pretender is long forgotten.

Still secrets

The curious shape of a whisky pot still evolved by trial and error as distillers became aware of its critical contribution to flavor. The dimensions of the onion-shaped copper pot, the fuel used to heat it, the length of its rising swan neck and the crucial angle of the lyne arm, which carries alcoholic vapors to the worm for condensation, are all vital.

Here, as in the art of malting barley, the human element can make or break a whisky. The stillman's skill and sharp eye decides the exact moment to capture the best of the distilled spirit, or "the heart of the run". "The stillman's job is one of great responsibility," former exciseman and whisky writer Neil Gunn wisely observed. "Negligence on his part may not only wreck the still but, what can hardly be detected at the time, ruin the flavour of the final spirit." (*Whisky in Scotland.*)

Aged in wood

Finally, there is the mystery of maturation. Single malts are invariably matured where they are made to allow local atmosphere to play its part. Experiments in shipping Scotch whiskies to the United States for maturation, or Highland malts to warehouses in Glasgow, have all concluded that the importance of place is inestimable.

As casks expand and contract with the changing seasons, the pores of the oak breathe, exhaling around 2 per cent of spirit per year (the "angels' share", which traditionally blackens the roofs of old maturation houses); while in the reverse motion, the wood "inhales" the mist, the fresh mountain air, or the seashore salt tang of its immediate environment. Moreover, the composition of the warehouse floor, the height and temperature at which casks are stored, and the method by which the stock is rotated also exert a significant influence.

The net result is whisky touched by nature, time and place. A spirit to be explored and contemplated in moments of quiet.

Types of whisky

Scotch whiskies may vary tremendously in style, character and quality but, like Kipling's Colonel's Lady and Judy O'Grady, they are nevertheless sisters under the skin.

Differences between single malts often invite comparison with the complexity of châteaux wines. For the novice, few experiences can be more daunting (or pleasurable) than to walk into, say, the Borestone Bar in Stirling and be confronted with 1,000 different malts, or the Lochside Hotel at Bowmore on Islay, where there are no less than 400 malts on display.

Where on earth do you begin? In negotiating what appears to be a malt whisky minefield, a useful step is to understand whisky's basic categories and production styles. In doing so, you may discover something to suit your palate and open up a world of choices.

It is worth remembering that the boldest drinkers reap the richest rewards. Whisky is a spirit not afraid to speak its mind. Never be timid about trying something new. Who knows, you may discover the dram of your dreams.

Single malt whiskies

These represent the fastest-growing market in the industry and more brands than ever are now available. Single malts, made from malted barley, are the distinctive product of one distillery. To maintain consistency of flavor and color, several casks of the same malt are vatted, or married, before bottling.

Single malts come in a bewildering array of ages. The lowest legally permitted age is 3 Years Old, (though most distillers consider 5 Years Old to be more acceptable), rising to 30 Years Old and upward. As with people, age does not automatically confer greatness or veneration. Single malts have an individual optimum age, after which they tend not to noticeably improve.

One school of thought holds that fifteen years in a cask is probably long enough for any whisky, though there are always exceptions. It is possible, for example, that an acclaimed 30 Years Old might have been better at 20 Years Old.

Grain whisky

This is distilled from various cereal grains – wheat, maize, barley – that have not been malted. The result is a fairly neutral spirit, of muted character, produced primarily for blending purposes. Grain whiskies, made in a Coffey still, provide the blank canvas for blends.

Single grain whiskies

These are bottled in small quantities by a handful of companies, including Old Cameron Brig, from Cameron Bridge, Fife, the world's first grain whisky distillery. The best examples often have a sweetish palate and rather more character than you might expect.

Vatted malts

These are single malt whiskies taken from different distilleries and blended to produce either a style typical of a particular region, or a combination of flavors that simply go well together. Vatting, like blending, broadens whisky's appeal by offering a palatable alternative for drinkers who dislike the assertive quality of some single malts.

Cask strength whiskies

These are closer to what a single malt tastes like at the distillery. They are sold at their original strength in the cask, around 60 per cent, rather than the normal practice of diluting to 40 per cent before bottling. Many drinkers prefer to add a few drops of spring water to a glass of cask strength whisky before tasting.

Cask strength malts are also different because, usually, they are not chill-filtered, that is passed through the refrigeration and filtration process that gives whisky its customary clarity. Cask strength malts may turn cloudy at low temperatures, but, on the other hand, they retain flavor elements normally removed by chill filtration.

Vintage single malts

Vintage single malts are a comparatively recent development, based on the oenological theory that certain years are outstanding, though whether this applies to whisky is open to debate. Certain batches of casks in dark corners of warehouses have been found to contain exceptional malts.

Vintages have their place and have certainly helped distillers to bring outstanding whiskies to public attention. However, the average single malt lover might be hard pressed to discern much difference, for instance, between a 1976 and a 1977 Laphroaig.

Wood finish single malts

Almost 70 per cent of whisky's characteristics come from wood. Maturation in American white oak barrels, formerly used to store bourbon, releases natural sweetness, while the charred interior filters undesirable flavors. Sherry butts, which are preferred by some distilleries, lend rich color and contribute a rounded sherry flavor. The Macallan is a wonderful example of the latter.

Each method leaves its individual fingerprint on a single malt. The type of cask in which a whisky is matured and the number of times it has been used make an enormous contribution to the character of the finished whisky.

A technique known as "finishing" has been perfected by Glenmorangie in a special range of Wood Finish Single Malts. These are matured initially for at least twelve years in American oak and then racked into casks, which previously contained, port, Madeira or sherry, for the final period of maturation. The experiment provides an interesting insight into the maturation process: the voluptuous flavor of whisky transferred to port pipes, the creamy influence of sherry and spicy notes from Madeira.

Single cask whiskies

This is the ultimate on the whisky scale, with a price guaranteed to leave a hole in your pocket, but, nevertheless, well worth it. Single malts, as we have seen, are vatted from a selection of casks to create consistency of color and flavor. A 10 Years Old malt comes from a single distillery, but is probably the product of many distillations, spread over a period of months. Single cask whiskies are, as they suggest, from a single cask, perfectly matured with all the individuality and idiosyncrasy that vatting is designed to smooth out.

A single cask whisky is the unique product of one distillation at a particular moment, a "snapshot" of a single malt. To confer on them the honor they deserve, single cask malts are usually numbered and beautifully packaged.

Blended whisky

This is what you probably buy the babysitter: a reasonably priced supermarket blend of grain and malt whiskies. However, blends have their own stratosphere of style. The better the blend, the higher the malt content. Many superior quality blends, such as Ballantines (who produce the world's most expensive blended whisky), the Johnnie Walker range or the lighter whiskies of Chivas Brothers and J&B are outstanding examples of the blender's art, with intriguing depths of aroma and flavor.

Surprisingly, although grain whiskies are very light in character compared with malts, their contribution is a positive one. At least two or three grains have to be used to give a blend its requisite balance.

Blended whiskies are by far the most popular style of Scotch whisky worldwide, accounting for at least 96 per cent of all whisky sales.

Right: Glenmorangie's wood finish range of single malts rounds off its maturation in sherry, port and Madeira casks.

How Malt Whisky is Made

"When you think there are only ninety distilleries in Scotland, and six out of those make malt by hand, that means there are only forty maltmen in the world and 200 mashmen. In fact, there are probably more astronauts than there are stillmen. These guys, the Donalds, the Anguses and Hughs, they are the elite."

Jim MacEwan, Morrison Bowmore Distillers

No other place of work quite resembles a whisky distillery: part engine room, part laboratory, part studio, it is an odd amalgam that reflects the multiple disciplines required of a distiller as he struggles to steer his handful of simple ingredients on a steady course.

In theory, whisky making is fairly simple. But working with natural elements is an unpredictable business. In fact, there are so many things that can go wrong with a whisky on its long march from grain to glass, that it's a wonder distillers manage to sleep at night.

Manufacturing the average 10 Years Old single malt demands the aptitude of an engineer, the mind of a biochemist and an artist's critical eye. Distilleries, with their spotless floors and whitewashed walls, are much more than factories where whisky is made. They are monuments to efficiency and pride of achievement.

It is no surprise that a nation of engineers and seafarers designed still rooms that were buffed and burnished like lighthouse lamp rooms. The distribution of cast iron tuns, wooden washbacks and copper stills – the flow pattern of production, linking each stage to the next – are often inspired expressions of logical thought.

Water

As transport improved, it became unnecessary for distilleries to be close to crops. What continued to influence their location, however, was proximity to a good supply of pure water. The spot where it bubbled from the ground, or the shining levels where it collected, dictated where whisky was produced. And, to a great extent, still does.

Thanks to Scotland's climate – 44 inches (112cm) of rainfall a year, compared to England's 31 inches (79cm) – and the catchment of its five-hundred million years old geology, Scotland has water in abundance. Soft or hard, peaty or crystal-clear, it fashions the character of malt whisky.

Curiously, Scotland's geology falls into areas which correspond broadly to its whisky regions: sandstone in the central and lowland areas filters water and contributes natural bicarbonates, while soft Highland water flowing over hard volcanic rock is almost pure rainwater. Sub divisions include Speyside and Scotland's oldest rocks, the ancient grists of western Islay.

A study in *Mining Journal* by consultant geologist Dr. Stephen Cribb and Julie Davison established a connection between rocks, water and the flavor of whisky, with detailed breakdowns relating types of rock to whisky brands. It appears that what water absorbs, or doesn't absorb, is only part of the story; the coolness of Scottish water is important, too, not just for condensing alcohol quickly, but, some believe, for influencing the flavor of the whisky.

"One Speyside loch has a temperature seldom rising above 10°C (50°F)," says Gordon Bell of Johnnie Walker, "it is freezing cold and the distiller considers this to be so important that he measures the temperature every morning".

The whole question of how individual water sources affect flavor is a subject of debate. Expert views range from that of connoisseur Michael Jackson who suspects it can be "overstressed and romanticized", to writer Philip Morrice who firmly believes that not only the type of water but its coolness affects the finished whisky.

Malting

The first task to which water is put is steeping the barley. Grain arrives at the distillery and each batch is carefully checked by the distiller. Today's barley differs from that used by Victorian whisky makers. Selective breeding has made it more disease resistant and the stems are considerably shorter to withstand battering in strong winds.

Despite the superiority of local Scottish barley, distillers also obtain supplies from France, England and Scandinavia, where harvests are earlier, to ensure a constant supply.

Because northern latitudes have a shorter growing season Scottish barley is ideal for whisky making; this brief period pressures the plant into producing more enzymes to convert natural sugars to starch. Later, at the distillery, these all-important enzymes are used to convert starch back to sugars, which in turn react with yeast to produce alcohol.

Don't feel too confused – the chemistry becomes clearer as we go along. The first crucial stage of whisky making occurs right at the beginning of the process, when ripe seed-heads of barley are soaked in local water in containers called steeps. After two or three days, the water is drained off and the wet seeds are spread on the stone floor of the malting house to a depth of about a foot (30cm).

The barley then begins to germinate, sprouting tiny roots and shoots and generating heat. Maltsters move methodically along the grain, turning it mechanically or by hand with wooden shovels, filling the maltings with a rich, sweet aroma. It is back-breaking work, but the rotation dissipates the warm air and prevents roots and shoots from tangling.

After about a week it is time to halt the germination of the "green", or growing, malt. This decision is taken at a precise time to capture an important enzyme called "diastase" which is responsible for making the natural starch in the seeds soluble. Ovens are then stacked with peat blocks and ignited with a twist of burning newspaper. Swirling smoke rises through a perforated iron platform over which the germinated barley has been spread, halting germination. The twenty-six compounds in peat smoke determine how much "peat reek", or smokey flavor, the finished whisky will have. The smoke finally emerges from the distinctive pagoda-shaped chimneys that dominate the distillery.

Traditional malting combines experience, judgement and instinct with science. It is a difficult process in which the maltman has to take many variables into account, from how much heat and smoke is given off by the glowing peat blocks, to wind direction and the stage germination has reached.

"Peating is a seat of the pants operation relying completely on time, temperature and experience," explains Alec Gunn, a maltings foreman for twenty-six years at Laphroaig, among the smokiest single malts. "Our recipe for kilning is eighteen hours exposure to peat reek, followed by about twelve hours on warm air. The temperature is never allowed to rise above 55°C (123°F) to protect the enzymes in the starch."

As heat and smoke bring down the moisture content of the barley from around 45 per cent to 4.5 per cent, the grain is imbued with a deliciously sweet, smokey character. The malted barley is cooled and stored for several weeks before shoots and rootlets are removed. The malt is then ground in milling machines, formerly water-driven, to reduce it to grist (hence the expression "grist to the mill"). The secret is a coarse consistency – if it is too fine the flavor of the whisky might change.

These days, only a tiny handful of distilleries have their own working maltings. Most barley is purchased ready malted

Mashing

The next stage of making whisky – mashing and fermentation – is collectively known as brewing. The effect of malting and milling was to break down large complex molecules of starch, cellulose and protein in the seed husks until they were small enough to become soluble in water. The coarsely milled malt, or grist, that resulted is now mixed with hot water in a large container known as a mash tun, which is covered like an enormous cooking pot to retain heat. (In the American whiskey industry, this process is known as "cooking".)

Inside the tun, paddles rotate and churn the mixture until it resembles a sloppy, richly smelling porridge. As it turns, it slowly becomes sweeter as natural starches in the malt convert to sugar. Mashing looks simple enough but within the swirling solution, sophisticated chemical reactions take place as three main sugars and forty-seven peripheral sugars are released.

The sweet liquor, or "wort", produced in mashing is drained off and fresh hot water added to the malt residue to extract all the fermentable sugar. Usually, the first two waters go on to make whisky, while the third kick-starts the next mashing session. When the wort has been drained from the mash tun after three or four fillings, the seeds and husks left steaming in the bottom ("draff", as distillers call it) are sold as malt-rich cattle feed.

Waste is one accusation that never can be levelled. Everything is put to good use, even surplus heat from the hot water. In Bowmore, on Islay, it keeps the local swimming pool warm; water at Glen Garioch (*glen geerie*) is harnessed to heat acres of greenhouse tomatoes; and at Tomatin there was an experiment to breed eels commercially.

Up to this point, the whisky-making process is very similar to brewing beer. Curiously, some distilleries use a mashing vessel called a "lauter tun". In Old German *lauter* referred to cleansing the blood, a term rooted in the days when ale was made by monks and was believed to be the elixir of life with powers to purify the soul.

Fermentation

After water and malted barley, yeast is the only other ingredient remaining in Scotch whisky. While local springs dictated the location of a still, barley and yeast influenced the time of year whisky was made. This had to be after the barley harvest, but before the weather became too warm, making yeast volatile and unpredictable to handle.

Fermentation takes place in containers called washbacks. Today these are mostly made in stainless steel, although washbacks built from Oregon pine, resembling giant wooden pails, are still common. First, however, the hot wort has to be cooled to around 22°C (71°F) before living yeast can be added.

"In the old days, when yeasts were less stable, fermentation could be extremely violent," whisky expert Charles MacLean explains. "Small boys were employed to fight back the foam with heather brooms." (*The Mitchell Beazley Pocket Whisky Book*.) Another writer compared the commotion to a ship caught in a storm.

Nowadays methods are slightly more sophisticated. Foam rises alarmingly high in the washbacks, but before it can overflow it is chopped by rotating blades, like scraping the head from a beer with a spatula. Carbon dioxide released during fermentation fills the tun room with sharp, fruity aromas reminiscent of jam making or home-brewed ale.

In fact, ale is what is being produced, a heady, cloudy brew of about 8 per cent alcohol by volume. The yeast responsible for the reaction is a pure culture, usually fresh for each fermentation and not allowed to contain additives or additional enzymes. The brewer keeps a watchful eye, monitoring the temperature in case it creeps too high and taints the finished

Distilling employs both science and the senses. Despite advances in technology, no machine has yet been built to rival the sophistication of the trained nose.

Left: Glenfiddich's huge mash tun is filled for another production batch. In this giant cooking pot complex sugars are released ready for fermentation.

Above: Careful checks are made at regular intervals of the alcoholic strength of whisky slumbering in the maturation sheds at Macallan.

whisky by giving a harsh edge to the taste. One of the rites of passage for first-time visitors to a distillery is sniffing the wash. The high concentration of carbon dioxide has a searing effect on the throat and nostrils, rather like inhaling paint-stripper.

Fermentation creates alcohol for the first time in the process, a point which heralds the appearance of the exciseman. From fermentation onwards, he takes a keen professional interest in the entire business of making whisky until it is bottled and sold. Distinguished excisemen have included the poet Robert Burns, the whisky writer Neil Gunn and

Maurice Walsh, the author of *The Quiet Man*.

In the past, not too much love was lost between distillers and "gaugers", as they were known. At Coleburn, near the Lossie, the owners expressed their feelings about the whisky tax in 1896 by "forgetting" to build the exciseman a lavatory. They relented, but only after eighteen months of pleading.

Following the era of illegal distilling, excisemen were posted in distilleries to ensure that not a single drop was unlawfully consumed before duty was paid. This was sometimes taken as a challenge. At Glen Albyn, home of a smokey Inverness malt, one determined local was deported to Australia for trying to outwit the exciseman. Officials discovered a pipe running from the spirit safe in the distillery still room, through the wall, to the pub next door.

Secrets of the pot still

The still room corresponds to most people's image of how whisky is made – sentinel rows of polished copper pots with swan necks rising as high as the roof. This is the heart of the process, where the wash is boiled and its alcoholic vapors captured and condensed, the moment when the thin "beer" produced from fermented wort becomes spirit.

Here, there is a sense of alchemy at work. The fact that alcohol has a lower boiling point than water has been known since ancient times, along with the importance of using copper vessels for their superior heat-conducting properties.

It is widely accepted that the shape of a still influences how light or heavy the finished whisky will be. From this grew the celebrated story of the dented still, about the distillery where an accidentally damaged still produced better whisky. From then on, the myth goes, replacement stills had to be made exactly in the image of the original, down to the last dimple.

Malt whisky thrives on such tales. However, the theory of still shape remains true. Tall stills (Glenmorangie boasts the tallest in the Highlands) produce lighter whisky. In a shorter still, chemical compounds, which create a heavier, oilier whisky, are carried over the top of the neck. In taller stills, they tend to fall back into the wash. A round bulge, or "boil pot", on the neck, just above the shoulder of the still, also indicates attempts to produce a lighter whisky.

There is a belief in Irish distilling that larger stills, with more cubic capacity for vapors to circulate, also make lighter whisky. Scottish distillers are more cautious. Some prefer to install additional stills of the same size, thereby increasing the distillery's overall capacity, than risk a change of flavor by introducing bigger vessels.

At the other end of the scale is an old distilling adage that the smaller the still, the finer the whisky. The most extreme example, which appears to bear the theory out, is that of The Edradour, near Pitlochry. Scotland's smallest distillery, with the whitewashed look of a Brigadoon backdrop and a staff of three, has miniature 500-gallon (2,273-litre/600-US-gallon) stills – the smallest allowed by law. Any smaller and they would be hidden away in the hillside, the manager says.

Pot distilling has changed little over the centuries. Alcohol vapor rises up the neck of the still to the point where, traditionally, it takes a right-angled turn to disappear outside the building. This short, near-horizontal length of neck is known

"The common belief that whisky improves with age is true. The older I get, the more I like it."

Comedian, Ronnie Corbett

as the lyne arm and its angle is believed to be important. Some lyne arms, like those at Cragganmore, make a straight, no-nonsense exit; others favor the downward departure of Glen Grant's or are set at an incline like those at Glencadam.

The idea was to convey the vapors outside the building into the cold air, where the lyne arm was connected to a coiled pipe, or "worm", immersed in cold water, contact with which quickly condensed the vapors.

Two stills are generally used: the wash still produces a spirit with an alcohol content of around 26 per cent. This unsophisticated distillate, called the "low wines", is then transferred to the spirit still to be redistilled, bringing the strength up to around 70 per cent. This is a critical part of the operation. Customs & Excise regulations prohibit any contact with the new spirit, which has to be controlled through a "spirit safe", resembling a fish-tank with a brass padlock.

The new spirit is directed and tested behind thick glass, an action not unlike swivelling a flowing hosepipe from one watering can to another. First, the stillman manipulates levers on the safe to set aside the "foreshots" – the initial part of the run – in a receiver. Next comes the "middle cut", the prime-quality heart of the whisky with an alcohol content of about 70 per cent. This is the spirit he carefully captures for his whisky. Eventually, as it becomes weaker, a lever is pulled to direct the third cut, the "feints", into another receiver. Both feints and foreshots are mixed with another batch of 26 per cent low wines, ready for the next distillation.

Despite the highly advanced technology of modern distil-

Left: Gleaming copper stills at Macallan. The necks ascend to join the lyne arms, which convey the spirit vapor into condensers.

Above: Single malts acquire their character during maturation. At Bruichladdich on Islay they absorb a faint whiff of ozone from the sea air.

leries, the traditional pot still, with its variables and uncertainties, is not the most accurate method of obtaining alcohol, but therein lies its charm. From its very imprecision, and reliance on manual skills, flows the wonderfully varied range of single malt Scotch whiskies that delight the world.

Ageing in wood

Scotch whisky is required to mature in wood for not less than three years, but many single malts are sold at their peak of 10 to 15 Years Old. Once bottled, whisky ceases to mellow, though some experts claim to have detected beneficial changes in bottled whiskies stored for long periods.

Almost like an undeveloped child, the flavor "genes" of the newly made whisky have been shaped by water, malting and distillation. But it is over the next few years, as the whisky ages, that the most fundamental changes take place. Almost 70 per cent of the characteristics of mature whisky are estimated to come from wood. Regardless of whether casks have previously been used for storing bourbon or sherry, the preferred wood for ageing is always strong, flexible oak.

The interior of American white oak bourbon casks are fired to char them. This releases vanillin (vanilla flavor) into first-fill bourbon, which, in turn, leaves taste traces when casks are later used for malt whisky. Sherry casks, which are spared such dramatic firing, reflect the rich color and sweetness of sherry. Around 95 per cent of the containers used by the Scotch whisky industry were formerly used for bourbon; about 5 per cent contained sherry.

However, this is only part of the fingerprint wood leaves on whisky. Compounds in the oak itself, such as tannins, sugars, oils and cellulose, are drawn into the new spirit as it matures. Obviously each cask has only a finite reserve. The more often it is used, the smaller the influence of these compounds, so careful records are kept of how many times a cask is filled.

As casks expand and contract, a reversal occurs: the charred interior acts as a filter, removing unwanted elements from the spirit. Evaporation, the fabled "angels' share", takes place at an annual rate of 2 per cent, equivalent to a gallon (4.5 litres/1.2 US gallons) a year. In general, spirit matures more quickly in smaller casks or at lower alcoholic strength. Most whiskies mature at 63.4 per cent alcohol by volume.

Finally, the warehouse itself plays an important part: tradition has it that cold, damp maturation sheds produce the best whisky, though this has never been scientifically proven. Scotland's temperate climate, with its unhurried seasonal changes, is ideal for the steady maturation of whisky. As the spirit slumbers, it absorbs something of the local atmosphere, such as the hint of the shoreline found in many Island malts.

Exploring Aromas

"What it really amounts to is this: a whisky is really enjoyable when it is good enough to be drunk at leisure."

Sir Compton Mackenzie

Ballantine's former Master Blender, Jack Goudy, had a nose that led him unfailingly to sniff out unwanted elements that, though undetectable to the rest of us, had crept into his whisky samples.

On one memorable occasion, he uncapped a sample of Balblair and instantly detected something different. He immediately rang the distillery manager, Jimmy Yates, to draw it to his attention. "Jimmy scratched his head," says Ballantine's Hector MacLennan, who relates the story. "There hadn't been any changes at Balblair that anyone could recall. A few buildings had been added up the hill in 1872. An extra still had been built in 1970, and that was about all. Then Jimmy remembered that he had had two feet of copper piping replaced in a section at the top of the still which led to the condenser. The new copper had been enough to minutely affect the flavor."

Smelling whisky gives us more information than our ability to detect the four basic tastes: bitter, sweet, salt and sour. The nose houses 1,000 tiny smell receptors, which pick up thirty-two primary aromas and thousands of permutations.

The two senses are closely interdependent: smell lends depth to taste and, of course, without smell there is no taste. To an experienced noser, almost half the enjoyment comes from whisky's complex aromas, though most would agree that the main pleasure is in the drinking.

Emotional aromas

Smell is closely linked to our emotions, arousing pleasurable sensations, warning of danger or, quite frequently, evoking memories by transporting us back in time. The smell of chalk can conjure up a classroom, pear drops a childhood corner shop, disinfectant a visit to hospital or cut grass a local playing field.

There is a belief that most of what we smell relates to childhood, or the distant past, and is often connected to pleasant or unpleasant experiences. When a whisky expert detects, say, butterscotch in the aroma of Glenfarclas or mint toffee in Aberlour, the framework for that identification is probably a childhood memory.

Ballantine's Master Blender Robert Hicks, a man with an incredible nose who can detect chlorine at one part per million in drinking water, subscribes to the theory. "Many of our taste memories are formed by the age of ten," he believes, "for example, Ballantine's 17 Years Old evokes memories of fresh red apples in an orchard in my childhood. Its hint of spiciness reminds me of sweets I ate on the way to school as a boy."

How our sense of smell works

Our olfactory system is triggered when tiny aroma particles contact a membrane of sensitive nerve fibers in the roof of the nose. These microscopic receptors pass messages to our cen-

Left: A sherry copita or tulip-shaped glass, such as this at Old Bushmills distillery, gathers the aroma of newly poured whisky for gentle nosing.

Below: Glenmorangie 18 Years Old was sent for appraisal to the expert noses at a New York perfume house and returned with surprising results.

tral "HQ" for analyzing smell – the olfactory "bulb" in the brain, which is close to the area that is associated with emotion and cognitive behavior.

Research at Chicago's Smell and Taste Foundation, perhaps the formost establishment in its field, indicates that women have a more finely tuned sense of smell than men, although in both sexes sensitivity declines slightly with age. (Despite this, our popular image of a seasoned whisky blender remains a white-haired male.)

The perfumiers' verdict

Single malt whisky contains an astonishing range of aromas contributed by the dry smokiness of peat, the sweetness of barley, the fruitiness of yeast and the huge influence of the cask, which passes on oakiness, sherry, vanilla, even sea air.

This was memorably demonstrated by Glenmorangie, a malt noted for its fragrant bouquet. Enthusiasts claimed to detect such a baffling range of aromas, and were so rarely in agreement, that the distillery decided to seek an objective opinion. A sample was sent to one of the most celebrated noses in the perfumery business, the legendary Christian St. Roche in Paris. To their surprise, he identified no fewer than twenty-six specific aromas in the whisky: from almond, bergamot and cinnamon to quince and vanilla, plus a host of other obscure elements, including peony, liquorice, mango, wild mint and ambergris.

Determined to unravel the riddle, Glenmorangie decided to investigate further. Bottles of 10 Years Old and 18 Years Old were dispatched to Belmay, the Long Island perfume house which creates 2,000 artificial essences for the perfume industry. Belmay's experts identified twenty-two different aromas in the 10 Years Old and seventeen in the 18 Years Old. Of these, only six overlapped and were found in both vintages, a clear indication that profound changes take place in whisky during its maturation.

In eight years, the aroma of the 10 Years Old had evolved: sharp lemon notes had been transformed to rounded orange, and those of apple, mint and banana to fuller plum and raisin flavors. Perhaps even more interesting was the fact that while Christian St. Roche and the Belmay experts collectively had the most sensitive noses in the business, the smells they identified were the same on only eight occasions.

From this, Glenmorangie concluded that their whisky contained core aromas of almond, apple, cinnamon, lemon, liquorice, mint, orange and vanilla. The wider conclusion was encouraging: nosing whisky is a highly personal, subjective exercise. Listen to the experts by all means, but never feel embarrassed to put forward your own opinion.

The language of whisky

Wine tastings are occasionally prone to descriptive flights of fancy, making them a target for cynics. James Thurber summed it up in a cartoon caption: "It's a naive domestic Burgundy without any breeding," one wine buff declares, "but I think you'll be amused by its presumption."

If, as Samuel Johnson suggested, language is the dress of thought, it is clear that some imbibers are attired more flamboyantly than others. As a nation, the Scots have tended to take a dim view of such verbal exuberance. There is an austere stratum of thought, from Highland bothy to Glasgow bar, that whisky is for drinking, not discussion.

Indeed, for most of its long history very few people have talked about it – sung its praises, certainly; penned a fair share of poetry, indeed, but rarely weighed its merits through objective discussion. One reason was that, for many years, whisky never had its own language.

In the 1970s as a consumer market for single malts grew, a need developed for whisky to have a sensible vocabulary, something to enable distillers and blenders to communicate with precision and clarity. It was felt that any new vocabulary should be rooted in plain English, not effusive metaphor.

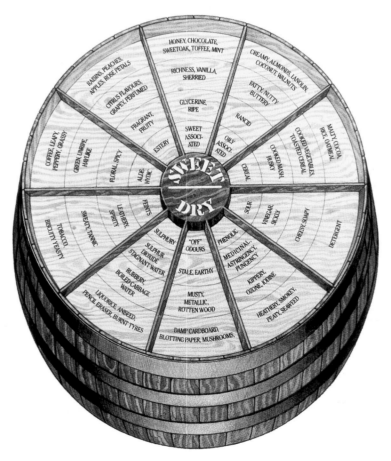

A basic whisky alphabet		
The team offered a new Scotch whisky alphabet of abstract terms, which included:		towards delicacy and fragrance.
		Mellow: well-matured – not too hot or pungent, but having a pleasant warming effect.
Bland:	lacking in "personality" or distinguishing characteristics.	**Rich:** high intensity of character compared to the whisky's standard flavor.
Clean:	free from off-notes, a term used mainly when tasting new whisky.	**Robust:** dominant flavor and aroma.
Dry:	an acceptable level of astringency.	**Round:** good balance of aroma and flavor notes.
Flat:	dull and flavorless, like lemonade that has lost its sparkle.	**Sharp:** imparting nose or mouth prickle.
Fresh:	the opposite of flat; ideal condition.	**Soft:** a comparative term used when pungency is subdued.
Hard:	metallic, flinty, an absence of delicate, sweet characteristics.	**Thin:** lacking the aroma and flavor it should have.
Heavy:	intensity of aroma and flavor.	**Young:** a whisky that has not reached its optimum stage of development.
Light:	good balance, tending	

Plain talking

In 1979 scientists at Pentlands Scotch Whisky Research, now the Scotch Whisky Research Institute, developed a flavor terminology in the then novel form of a wheel. Around the hub were aromatic compounds found in whisky, such as fusil oils (feints), aldehydes, esters and wood effects, and, radiating from them like spokes, fairly down-to-earth taste descriptions. Until then, whisky makers had borrowed terms haphazardly from brewing and wine production.

The Pentlands Flavour Wheel, however, while it filled an obvious need within the industry, was considered not to be "user friendly" for consumers.

A few years later, in the 1980s, whisky connoisseur John D. Lamond set to work with Aberlour Distillery to reinvent the wheel. The result was something more accessible to the average whisky drinker with an urge to explore. Following the wheel, the further out from the hub, the more complex the characteristics became. The Aberlour Malt Whisky Wheel stimulated an interest in malt whisky tasting, but, sadly, in the way of many marketing campaigns, faded away after a comparatively short period.

The most dedicated attempt to bring the message of malt whisky's delights to the masses largely fell to the pioneering work of the writer Michael Jackson, who set about tasting

Left: The sadly defunct Aberlour Tasting Wheel, conceived as more user-friendly to the average whisky drinker than the Pentlands version.

Right: Scientists came up with the Pentlands Flavour Wheel, with its precise taste definitions, in an attempt to standardize language.

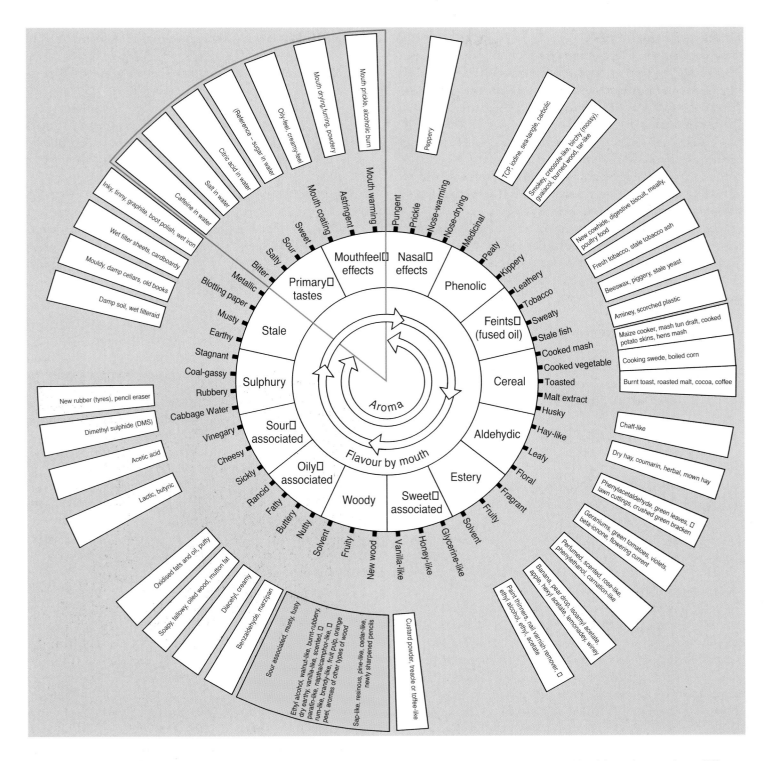

whiskies with freshness and enthusiasm. In the late 1980s Jackson became the first writer to systematically taste and assess malt whiskies, evaluating their qualities with a points system, singing their praises and opening hitherto unexplored areas of pleasure. More importantly, he achieved this in a language that managed to be both everyday and elegant.

"The Pentlands Flavour Wheel is trying to do a different job, something much more analytical", he says. "It is not telling the consumer what pleasurable experiences you can get from a whisky. That is what I am trying to do. In a hundred years time, I hope someone will simply say 'Thanks for telling us what it tasted like'."

Whisky and food

Cooking with whisky has been one of Scotland's best-kept secrets. The joys of Scotland's rich, natural larder, coupled with the secrets of adding a splash of single malt to cooking are increasingly being discovered south of the Border.

French masterchef Albert Roux was a pioneer of cooking with whisky, using Old Pulteney to flavor a black pudding appetizer at his London restaurant, Le Gavroche. His choice of whisky for this dish came from the most northerly distillery on mainland Britain, a malt that is nicknamed the "Manzanilla of the North" for its salty tang.

Other bravehearts have since followed suit, including Andy Barber at the Michelin-starred The Fulham Road. For a United Distillers Burns Night, his menu featured United Distillers' Six Classic Malts which demonstrate the versatility of cooking with whisky. His canapé-style first courses offered a choice of:

Glazed Scotch oysters with tagliolini pasta
and Dalwhinnie sabayon

•

Wild organic Glenarm salmon marinated in Cragganmore
with dill and smoked horseradish sauce

•

Oban-infused barley and apple risotto
with caramelized foie gras

•

Black Angus beef topside cured with Talisker
and aromatic spices.

This was followed by Roast Scotch Teal with Glenkinchie, served with white faggots and highland mushrooms and, for anyone with room to spare, warm, spiced Lagavulin pudding with malted iced parfait.

Cooking with whisky is wonderful for reviving jaded taste buds and enhancing the flavors of food, but there are a couple of rules of thumb worth considering. Catherine Brown, the author of several books on Scottish cuisine, believes that malt whiskies are more effective as a flavoring than a cooking ingredient, but this is a view not necessarily shared.

One common-sense guide is to match food and spirits of similar "weight". A light, delicate dish, for example, might

Smoked salmon – wild as opposed to farmed, if you can get it – is a superb accompaniment to peaty single malts. The best Scottish smoke houses not only produce a heavier flavor than counterparts from Canada and Europe, but also cure salmon individually over glowing whisky-barrel chips.

lend itself to the subtlety of a Lowland malt. Full-bodied whiskies make a better match with bold, robust dishes.

Chef Alan Hill's rule of thumb is that the heartier or more rustic the food, the stronger the peat flavor should be in the whisky you settle for. Of United Distillers' Six Classic Malts, he recommends soft, Lowland Glenkinchie for poultry or soups; light, aromatic Dalwhinnie with desserts; slightly more peaty Oban with fish or lamb; forest-distilled Cragganmore for the more robust flavors of lighter game; Talisker from the Isle of Skye with seafood; and earthy Lagavulin for red meats.

"Once you have tried cooking with Scotch, it will no longer be a novelty," Alan Hill says. "Most likely you will want to move it from the spirits pantry by the home bar to the spices and flavorings cupboard in the kitchen, making it an integral part of your cuisine."

Below: Whisky and good food have long been complementary. In recent years matching individual malts with dishes has been increasingly explored.

Butterscotch Cheesecake

Cookery writer Margaret Ashby has visited every distillery in Scotland to spread the message of whisky and food. This is one of her favorite whisky puddings.

Butterscotch Sauce Ingredients
4oz (125g) unsalted butter
4oz (125g) demerara sugar
10fl oz (300ml) condensed milk

Cheesecake Base Ingredients
approximately 8oz (225g) semisweet biscuits
butter, softened

Cheesecake Topping Ingredients
8 oz (225g) low-fat soft cheese
2 tablespoons double cream
half of the Butterscotch Sauce
whisky to taste (preferably Linkwood for this recipe)
fresh fruit or chopped nuts and grated bitter chocolate, for
  topping

Method
To make the butterscotch sauce, place all the sauce ingredients in a saucepan over a low heat and, stirring all the time, cook until golden brown. Store in the refrigerator until needed. This recipe makes double quantity, but it will keep for several days and is also delicious over vanilla ice cream with a little malt whisky added.

To make the cheesecake base, crush the biscuits with enough softened butter to stick the crumbs together. Line a dish with the mixture.

To make the cheesecake mixture, blend together the low-fat soft cheese, double cream and half of the Butterscotch Sauce and add whisky to taste. Pour the cheesecake mixture over the biscuit base.

Top with fresh fruit, or with chopped nuts and grated bitter chocolate in equal quantities.

Nosing & Tasting

"I keep six honest serving-men
(They taught me all I knew);
Their names are What and Why and When
And How and Where and Who."

Rudyard Kipling (1865–1936)

Towards the end of 1992, the British off-licence chain Oddbins ran a tasting day to widen the appeal of malt whiskies. The advertisement promised that anyone who dropped in could sample the delights of "jetty sheds, oily ropes, rotting bladder-wrack, Dundee marmalade and even dead hedgehogs" if they tried a dram of Lagavulin, Laphroaig, Talisker, Highland Park, Glenkinchie, Dalwhinnie, Bunnahabhain, The Balvenie, Oban, Bowmore, Aberlour and Cragganmore, more or less in that order.

The tongue-in-cheek promotion underlined the bewildering complexity of language in tasting. Islay's more pungent malts, for example, may be described as phenolic by some, peaty by others or reminiscent of diesel and hospital gauze.

Tasters methodically work their way through a whisky's color, aroma, body, flavor and finish, noting what they deduce from each. There is no substitute for conducting your own tastings and keeping your own notes. Compare them with the experts' views, but remember that they sometimes have differing impressions themselves.

Organizing a tasting

Glassware is important: for serious tasting, put your favorite cut-glass tumbler away. You need something to gather aromas rising from the surface of the spirit: a *copita* sherry glass is ideal, but a brandy balloon, thistle glass or anything that narrows slightly at the top will do. To focus the aroma, cover the glass with a watch-glass or a piece of paper when not in use.

Setting up the glasses on a white tablecloth provides a good background for examining color. Some tasters recommend a plate of crusty bread to cleanse the palate between malts, or a glass of water to refresh the mouth. A pad and pen are invaluable to note your observations, particularly if you are tasting several whiskies. The fun of keeping a record is to go back to the same brands at a later date and compare your observations. Knowledge should expand with experience.

Lastly, have a bottle of soft, still Scottish spring water to hand, ideally from the region where the whisky was produced, to dilute the whisky and release its aromas. Tap water will do, providing it is soft and does not contain too much chlorine. Like the whisky, it should be cool but not refrigerated. Ignore any advice about trying single malts with ice; cold whisky shuts down its aromas, as well as freezing the taste buds.

Color

Your first impression will be of color. This may vary from a shade as pale as sunrise (colorless, if it's from the Isle of Man), through straw, gold, amber and mahogany, to the jet black of double-charred Loch Dhu, the darkest of all single malts.

Color offers clues as to how a whisky has matured. Young spirit draws its hue from the wood as it ages. It may emerge from bourbon white oak, for instance, a shade of almond, and from sherry butts, a variety of rich colors up to ruby and mahogany. Whisky matured in a mixture of bourbon barrels and sherry casks can be somewhere between the two, a pleasant gold or amber.

How many times the cask has previously been filled can also influence color: "second fill" casks (or third or fourth fill) produce less intense coloring. In the end, appreciation comes down to aesthetics – any color that appeals to you looks wonderful against the light.

Tilt your glass to wet the sides, then straighten it. The "tears" of whisky travel to the bottom at different rates, depending on the character of the malt. The faster they head towards the bowl of the glass, the lighter the whisky style. Heavy, intense malts often move with the slowness of treacle.

Nosing

Remove the cover from your glass and give the whisky a sniff. Don't stick your nose in too far and don't inhale so deeply that the alcohol anaesthetizes your nasal passages. Just a gentle whiff to gather your first impression.

The professionals who invented the Pentlands Flavor Wheel allocated space to nasal effects: "pungent", "nose-prickling", "nose warming", "nose drying" and "peppery". Any prickling or burning indicates a strongly flavored whisky.

Now add a splash of still spring water and note the differ-

ence. Forget the "real-men-take-it-neat" theory: water loosens and relaxes whisky, releasing fruity esters and floral aldehydes and expanding its aromas. Tasters refer to these subtle fragrances as "notes". For whiskies bottled at "normal" strength, i.e. 40 to 43 per cent alcohol by volume, add up to a third water, according to taste (fifty-fifty if it suits you better). Stronger and cask-strength whiskies require a little more.

First impressions are important. They tell you what you like about a particular malt. Follow your intuition: if you think it smells like a newly mown cricket pitch, or seaweed on the beach, jot it down. Blenders and distillers may talk technically about feints and phenols but whisky is also a highly enjoyable experience; explore the memories it arouses.

A good tip from Allied Distillers master blender Robert Hicks: once you have noted your first impressions, put them as far out of your mind as you can and nose again. With practice, another layer will reveal itself. Robert likens it to removing the various skins of an onion (minus the smell!) to delve deeper into the whisky.

Tasting

Take a generous slurp and let it roll leisurely over the tongue and round the sides of your mouth. The first thing to strike you is the texture of the whisky, sometimes known as "mouth-feel", or body. Does it coat your mouth with an oily or creamy feeling? Does it dry your mouth in an astringent manner? Does it make your mouth feel warm? The body of a malt may be light, full, soft, firm, smooth, even sticky, and is an important component of its style and character.

The palate of a whisky is its flavor – quite literally its taste – as the palate forms a division between the mouth and the nose, our center of smell. As you detect a particular flavor, notice how it acquires a different dimension depending on whether it is on the tip of the tongue (sweetness), the sides (saltiness and sourness), or the back of the tongue (dryness and bitterness).

After primary tastes of sweet, sour, salty and bitter, flavors may range from medicinal to tobacco, toast, hay, flowers, honey (follow the Pentlands Flavor Wheel). Or in the simpler language of the Aberlour Wheel: cereal, floral, fruity, leathery, etc. Consider whether flavors balance nicely, or if some dominate others. Does it "go down singing hymns", as one taster said of Glenfarclas, or fighting all the way?

The "finish" simply refers to how long the flavor lasts – the sensations you pick up a minute or two after swallowing. With some whiskies, you hope it will be forever, and some do linger longer than others before they fade and bid farewell. Remember, practice makes perfect.

The whisky regions

The first attempt to divide Scotland into distinct whisky regions was made, not by distillers or whisky lovers, but by London legislators who drew up the 1784 Wash Act, creating Highland and Lowland excise regions for collection purposes.

However, nature had already beaten Customs and Excise officials to it. The kind of water and peat used and the geographical locations of distilleries conspired to produce recognizable styles of whisky from different parts of Scotland. How this came about is as mysterious as the wine regions of France with their differing soils, grape varieties and exposure to sunlight.

Traditionally, Scotland has been loosely divided into four whisky areas: Highlands, Lowlands, Campbeltown and Islay. In the last century blenders went further and defined them as North Country, Lowland, Campbeltown, Islay and Glenlivet. But even that wasn't quite straightforward. Some single malts seem to be situated on the wrong side of dividing lines, while others curiously display characteristics of regions that are some distance away.

Highland single malts

Highland whiskies hail from north of a diagonal line running from Greenock and Dumbarton on the Firth of Clyde in the west, to Perth and Dundee on the River Tay in the east. Geographically, it is the biggest region, though by no means has the most distilleries. Within it lies the legendary Speyside area, into which around half Scotland's single malt distilleries are shoe-horned. Vast tracts of the Highland region have no distilleries at all. Above Fort William, for instance, there is only Talisker on Skye and none on the whole western mainland.

The Highland landscape, whose rugged terrain can be at once breathtaking and foreboding, with weather which may switch from sunshine to storm within minutes, produces whiskies as changing as its character.

On the whole, they tend to be refreshingly robust, well-rounded malts, dry and slightly peaty. But there are wide variations: the region embraces islands and coastal distilleries (Scapa, Clynelish, Talisker, Oban, Jura) which smack of the shoreline and sea air. The northern Highlands, Europe's most sparsely populated wilderness, has aromatic, spicy, bitter-sweet single malts (Balblair, The Dalmore, Teaninich, Glenmorangie) with character borrowed from crisp, crumbly peat.

Whiskies from the eastern and midland areas (The Edradour, Aberfeldy, Fettercairn, Glencadam), sheltered from the excesses of westerly weather, have more expansive fruit-and-nut flavors with a pleasing sweetness.

Towards the Lowland line, but still technically in the Highlands (Deanston, Glenturret and Tullibardine near Perth), the style becomes lighter, smoother, more medium-bodied with a fresh flavor.

Lowland single malts

South of the Lowland line, the countryside is gentler, the hills settling into a soft eiderdown – qualities expressed in the light, mellow, less-challenging single malts of the region's distilleries.

High duties in the early eighteenth century forced Lowland distilleries to mix cheaper, unmalted grain with their barley. "A most rascally liquor", Burns termed it. As a result, Lowland whisky was inevitably contrasted with fuller Highland malts which became a byword for integrity. The good name of Lowland malts has long since been restored. While softer and more understated than their emphatic, hairy-kneed Highland counterparts, they are not without character of their own – fragrant and floral with restrained fruity notes. Traditionally, many were triple distilled, though the only examples of this style now are Auchentoshan and Rosebank.

Lowland malt whiskies have an aperitif quality; a refreshing, often zesty personality that makes them ideal for any occasion (particularly clean-tasting Auchentoshan, grassy Glenkinchie and Littlemill, a delightful pick-me-up from one of Scotland's oldest distilleries).

Like Campbeltown, the influence of Lowland whisky has diminished. There was a time when every town in the region was said to have a distillery; now only four remain operational.

Below: The Western Highlands with the Isle of Skye behind. This rugged, windswept region is home to a charful collection of single malts.

Right: The high remote Cairngorms, where great whisky rivers, such as the Spey and the Avon, begin their journey to the North Sea.

Speyside

Speyside single malt whiskies are regarded as the jewel in the crown of the Scotch whisky industry. Elegant, fruity, *premier cru* malts, balanced by a nice dry smokiness.

Around forty-seven distilleries cluster around the system of rivers which flow through this triangle of the eastern Highlands. Climb Ben Rinnes above Aberlour distillery on a clear day, it is claimed, and you can count forty-three of them.

Speyside distilleries cling to a river system flowing in roughly parallel formation to the North Sea between Aberdeen and Inverness. The region is bounded to the west by the River Findhorn and, to the east, by the River Deveron, but a number of distilleries falling outside this unofficial area claim the coveted Speyside appelation.

The acknowledged heart of Speyside is the famous glen of the River Livet, home to three outstanding malts: Braes of Glenlivet (which is used entirely for blending in Chivas Regal and unavailable for tasting), Tamnavulin and The Glenlivet itself, the only malt entitled to use the name. The Glenlivet has acquired such a gigantic reputation for balance and elegance that many distilleries beyond the tiny glen tack Glenlivet onto their name.

Speyside malts are characterized by a delicate subtlety, often light and perfumy (as in Tamdhu, Knockando or the monumental Glen Grant); the breathtaking grace and drinkability of The Glenlivet and Glenfiddich, and the impressive depth and complexity of whiskies like Linkwood and Cragganmore. At the other end of the Speyside scale are a cluster of outstanding sherried malts, including The Macallan, Aberlour, Glendronach and Glenfarclas.

With practice (and frequent tasting!) it becomes fairly easy to identify Speyside malt whiskies by their sheer quality, and to understand why they give Scotch whisky a reputation for distinction that has never been equalled.

Campbeltown

"The deepest-voiced of all the choir", as one devotee eulogized, Campbeltown, with two distilleries producing three whiskies, is still recognized as a whisky region (just). While at one time it had an heroic reputation for bold whiskies of character, consistency nose-dived somewhat between the two world wars. Around thirty distilleries worked overtime supplying America's thirsty masses during Prohibition. It was not the most discerning market and the Mull of Kintyre, well placed for Atlantic shipments, accepted the challenge, often with more of an eye for profit than quality.

Today's Campbeltown malts, which have never compromized, have substantial body and a dry, smokey character (prominent in Longrow, made at Springbank) with salt-air notes to the fore in Springbank and Glen Scotia.

Islay (*eye-la*)

Islay, in the Inner Hebrides, is associated with the pungent, big-bodied, peaty malts of its southern shore: Laphroaig, Lagavulin (*lagga-voolin*) and Ardbeg. In fact, its nine distilleries produce smokey, seaweedy malts that vary enormously in intensity: Bruichladdich (*brew-ick-laddy*), Scotland's most westerly distillery, for instance, pales beside its heavier neighbors; and Bunnahabhain (*boon-a-havan*), from the east, has been described as a malt lacking Islay character). Between these extremes lie the beautifully balanced Bowmore and Caol Ila (*cuu-eela*), which has a pleasantly assertive peatiness.

A tasting tour of Scotland

"Savoring that first sip, I wondered where my journey would take me..."

Dalwhinnie distillery manager Bob Christine on his first tasting tour of West Highland malt whisky in 1965

One of the most pleasurable ways to explore Scotland's distinctive whisky regions is by armchair, slowly sipping your way on a journey of discovery. In the late 1980s, United Distillers, owners of twenty-seven single malt distilleries, carefully selected six malts which they believed typify each of the regional styles. The Six Classic Malts are among the most familiar labels on supermarket shelves. They make convenient staging posts on a journey round the whisky regions.

Glenkinchie 10 Years Old (43% vol) has all the persona of a typical Lowland malt: smooth and softly aromatic. Of these sweetish regional malts, it ranks among the smokiest and has the slight dryness of a fine sherry. The distillery lies a short drive from Edinburgh, where Glenkinchie was traditionally well suited to sophisticated urban tastes.

The Kinchie Burn, fed by waters from the Lammermuir Hills, meanders between lush green banks which somehow lend character to this gentle malt. It has a soft, grassy aroma, reflecting a landscape a long way from the harsh extremes of the Highlands. Only available as a self in recent years, but summing up the Lowland style with great sophistication and deserving of its acclaim.

Dalwhinnie 15 Years Old (43% vol) hails from the central Highlands but, perhaps because of its elegant smoothness, is often classified as a Speyside malt, despite lying more than twenty miles (32km) outside the region's accepted boundaries. Dalwhinnie's influences owe more to the Highlands with its heathery notes and fruity aroma. The distillery, on the cold, windswept moors of the Grampians, is one of the highest in Scotland and uses snow-melted water. The resulting style is clean, light and rather dry with a heather-honey finish. A surprisingly gentle whisky considering its harsh environment.

Cragganmore 12 Years Old (40% vol) is a superb example of the firm-bodied, graceful whiskies for which Speyside is famous. In its time it has been hailed as a masterpiece and in Michael Jackson's view it has the most complex nose of all the malts. Its unique qualities come in part from the water, which is considered fine enough to be bottled for its own merits and

Below: A characterful bunch – the six Classic Malts from United Distillers, chosen to sum up the diverse qualities of Scotland's whisky regions.

Right: The six Classic Malts series whiskies typify the style of Scotland's whisky regions. Half have a strong coastal influence of peat and sea air.

piped to distillery workers' homes. Cragganmore's two spirit stills have an interesting flat top in place of the usual swan neck, which causes a reflux whereby heavier compounds are forced back into the pot. The result is a finely balanced malt with tremendous depth and a malty, smokey finish.

Oban 14 Years Old (43% vol) is a coastal, West Highland malt, influenced in equal part by both Highland and Island styles, which is exactly what you would expect, considering its position – the distillery sits with its back to the hills, facing the westerlies that howl in from the Inner Hebrides.

Oban distances itself from the Islands with a delicate peatiness, while its maltiness and fruity undertones smack of the Highlands. The distillery warehouse on the shore lends a suitably nautical note during maturation. Draw the cork and you can almost hear the seagulls. A beautiful balance of styles.

Talisker 10 Years Old (45.8% vol) comes from Skye's only distillery and has a highly individual style, quite unlike any other. Some tasters have remarked on Talisker's hot, peppery

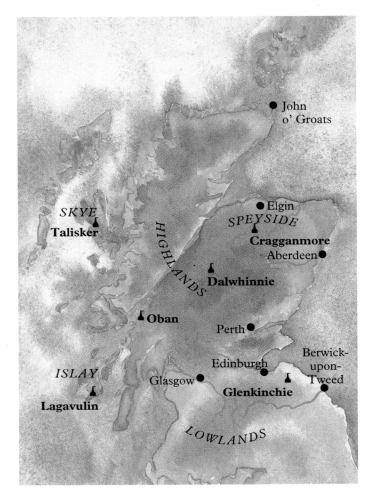

intensity and the way it "explodes" on the palate. It has a full body, a finish that goes on forever and a character of strong iodine and seaweed notes, drawn heavily from the sea.

Despite its roistering assertiveness, it is not a heavy malt but well-balanced and capable of surprises, not least among them a smokey sweetness to soothe the hot glow. The perfect pick-me-up after a winter walk.

Lagavulin (*lagga-voolin*) 16 years Old (43% vol) is a heavyweight Islay malt perched at the opposite end of the scale to lightweight Glenkinchie of the Lowlands. Between these extremes lie all the subtle variations of Highland and Speyside style – the great girth of flavor that makes up Scottish single malt whiskies.

Lagavulin emphatically captures the character of Islay, covered with a thick mantle of peat and lashed by sea winds. This pungent, robust, full-bodied malt is among the driest you could hope to encounter, perfectly counterbalanced with a wave of sherry sweetness and a suggestion of the shoreline.

The giants

While some single malts typify a particular regional style, others simply represent themselves. In their own way they have become legends among whisky connoisseurs. Try them, get to know them, and explore what sets them apart.

For the best part of a century it has become a pastime of Scotch whisky experts to compile their own favorite chart of the best single malts. In 1930 Aeneas Macdonald nominated twelve monumental malts in his classic book *Whisky*: The Glenlivet, Glen Grant, Highland Park, Glenburgie, Cardhu, Balmenach, Royal Brackla, Glenlossie, Longmorn, The Macallan and Linkwood. The twelfth was a split decision between Clynelish and Talisker.

In *Whisky in Scotland* (1935) former exciseman and poetaster Neil Gunn opted for Glen Mhor (*glen vor*) and Old Pulteney. David Daiches expressed a preference for Glenmorangie, Dalmore, Glen Mhor, Linkwood, Longmorn, The Glenlivet, Glen Grant and The Macallan. Michael Jackson, with his unique scoring system, awards the maximum points to Lagavulin.

Despite the wonderfully subtle array of flavors on offer, my own preference is a bottle of liquid smoke lashed by the wild sea at Laphroaig. Although single malts display so many admirable attributes of balance, elegance, fragrance or the delicacy of sherry ageing, in the end it comes down to personal taste. Which explains something about why the world is a wonderful place and Scotch whisky the perfect spirit to accompany it.

A Single Malt Guide

Speyside Malt Whisky

*"There is no common quality that infuses all
the Speyside malts except quality itself.
They are the aristocrats of whisky, many with
lineages going back into the mists of Scottish history."*

Brian Murphy, *The World Book of Whisky*

The Spey is as impressive as the whiskies created on its fertile plains.
Scotland's second river, rich in salmon and trout, is the fastest flowing in
Britain. It rises in tiny Loch Spey, near the Corrieyairach Forest, deep in the
"irksome solitude" of the Monadhliath, the Grey Mountains, to flow
through some of Scotland's most beautiful scenery into Spey Bay.

Despite so many single malt distilleries being crammed into Strathspey,
few use Spey water, preferring instead to draw supplies from adjoining
burns and springs.

If Speyside is Scotland's whisky heartland, its sanctum sanctorum is the
Glenlivet region, a name so synonymous with quality that, at one time,
almost thirty distilleries borrowed the name to hyphenate with their own.
Only The Glenlivet single malt is entitled to the appellation.

Speyside malts vary enormously within the region, from quite heavy and
sherried to medium, fruity malts and those of a light-bodied floral nature. A
congregation of highly individual, stylish whiskies united in quality and elegance. Twenty years ago, half were used only within the industry for blending. Almost all the Speyside malts are now available, enabling whisky lovers
to explore a unique region in all its glory. We examine them glen by glen as
distilleries follow the course of Speyside's eight main rivers.

*Right: The fast-flowing Spey, just
before it turns at Grantown to enter
Strathspey, home of many famous
Speyside distilleries.*

The Malts of Glen Livet

Only four distilleries can lay geographical claim to this exclusive glen. Of them, only The Glenlivet and Tamnavulin lie on the diminutive River Livet itself, which joins the Avon (*a'an*) to flow into the Spey. Looking down from the hills is Seagram's Braes of Glenlivet distillery, making an unbottled malt used exclusively for blending.

The surrounding hills were a traditional haven for illicit distilling, plentiful in peat, barley and pure water. As with other Speyside glens, the grouping does not denote a distinctive style, but suggests grace, depth and balance of flavor.

THE GLENLIVET

George Smith, son of a raffish whisky smuggler, took out the first distillery licence under the 1824 Act. His landlord, the Duke of Gordon, was a prime mover in persuading the government to encourage legal distilling. However, George found the legitimate life far from easy – violent attacks by local bootleggers forced him to pack a pair of hair-trigger pistols.

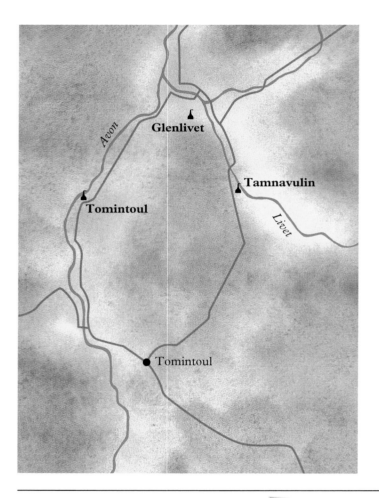

Below: Worm-tubs for condensing spirit vapor tower over a cottage at The Glenlivet distillery in 1890. (Illustrated London News).

Above right: The Glenlivet distillery today, home of a single malt with a proud history and probably the first to take out a licence.

THE GLENLIVET

Owner:	Seagram
Age:	12 years; 40%
Color:	Old gold
Aroma:	Exquisitely balanced with a delicate array of floral and honey-sweet notes that make it one of the most elegant single malts.
Taste:	Fragrant and fruity sweet, beautifully offset by malty dryness. Slides into a smooth, gentle finish. A class act.
Comment:	Acknowledged as one of the greats for 170 years. Ideal for any occasion and always sure to please.

TAMNAVULIN

Owner:	White & Mackay
Age:	10 years (no age statement); 40%
Color:	Pale straw
Aroma:	Light and fragrant. Elegant and refined with soft, floral, grapey notes.
Taste:	Dry and firm. Clean on the palate with pleasant grassy notes and a slightly smoky finish.
Comment:	Its light, almost zesty appeal makes it ideal as an aperitif.

Tamnavulin – "the mill on the hill" in Gaelic – stands in the village of Tomnavulin (different spelling) and takes its water both from the Livet and a local spring. The result is a smooth, sweet malt which is very individual, despite the daunting shadow cast by its neighbor.

TOMINTOUL (*tom-in-towel*)

Another modern distillery which recorded its first distillation in 1965. Reputedly Scotland's highest distillery (a claim challenged by Dalwhinnie) and often cut off by snow in winter. Tomintoul revives a long local distilling tradition – in 1800 the village was described as a place where "everyone made whisky and everyone drank it".

The water supply from Ballantuan spring was cautiously monitored and analyzed for two years before the decision to build was taken. Tomintoul-Glenlivet, which has a light, fresh edge, was first bottled in the early 1970s and is widely used in White & Mackay blends.

Right: The Glenlivet's unassuming label and packaging conceal a whisky of exquisite balance and stature which has won friends worldwide.

By 1880, the distillery had developed such a reputation for producing a mellow whisky combining full flavor and delicate aroma that a host of would-be imitators impeded business. The company sought legal protection to safeguard its name. As a result, a court ruled that only the Smiths could call their malt The Glenlivet.

Balance has since become a byword. The distillery's water, drawn from Josie's Well, is fed by both soft and hard springs; the malt used is a combination of light and heavily peated. Eight stills produce 1,200,000 gallons (5,300,000 litres/1,400,000 US gallons) annually.

The fame of The Glenlivet probably spread faster than any other single malt, and deservedly so. Sales soared after acquisition by Seagram in 1978 to make it the biggest selling 12 years old single malt in the world.

TAMNAVULIN (*tam-na-voo-lin*)

A modern, efficient distillery built at the mouth of the glen in 1966 on the site of an old woollen mill now incorporated into the visitors' center.

TOMINTOUL

Owner:	White & Mackay
Age:	12 years; 40%
Color:	Gold
Aroma:	Light, with a touch of sweetness and a summery fragrance.
Taste:	A smooth, slightly creamy body with great bursts of distinguished flavor. A nice balance of peat and sweetness and a long, spicy finish.
Comment:	Merchant and connoisseur Wallace Milroy recommends Tomintoul-Glenlivet as a good entry-level malt. Among the lightest from the Glenlivet area.

Glenfiddich & its Neighbors

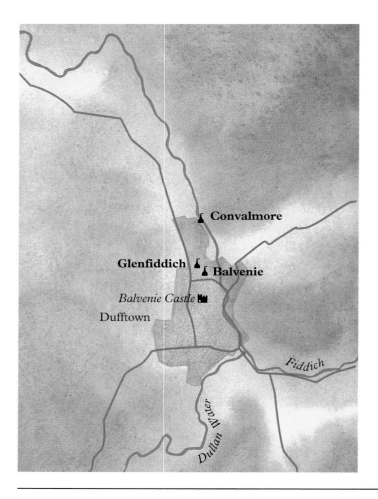

"Glenfiddich is not large, nor is it of ancient lineage, but I doubt if as much highland grit and guts were ever put into the building of any other distillery"

Sir Robert Bruce Lockhart, *Scotch*

There's a saying that just as Rome was built on seven hills, Dufftown was built amid seven stills. The original distilleries, built between 1823 and 1898, were Glenfiddich, Balvenie, Convalmore, Parkmore (closed in 1931), Dufftown, Mortlach and Glendullan. These days, the number is higher with the addition of Pittyvaich in 1975 and Kininvie in 1992, neither of which are bottled at the time of writing.

Dufftown, where the River Fiddich joins the Dullan Water, is a hilly, stone-built little town steeped in whisky and surrounded by famous distilleries. The most celebrated is Glenfiddich, home of the world's best-selling malt.

William Grant was born in Dufftown in 1839, the poor son of a soldier who left school early to provide for the family. He worked at Mortlach distillery for twenty years, nursing a dream to make his own whisky. His chance came to realize this dream when some old distilling equipment was put up for sale and he bought it for £120.

He built Glenfiddich distillery with his bare hands and the help of his sons. When it opened in 1886 his three sons continued to educate them-

GLENFIDDICH

Owner:	William Grant & Sons
Age:	No statement; 40%
Color:	Pale gold
Aroma:	Natural, fresh and fragrant with few dominant notes.
Taste:	Crisp, dry and delicately balanced. Soft on the palate with an exceptionally smooth, lingering finish.
Comment:	A gentle malt of great poise and elegance – ideal for anyone making the transition from blended whisky to selfs.

Left: Glenfiddich's distinctive triangular bottle was introduced in 1957. The company followed with another first – the cardboard tube.

Above: Balvenie Castle, where the annual rent was once a single red rose. Glenfiddich's sister distillery, the Balvenie, is nearby.

selves, and books on Latin and maths were commonly found scattered around the tun-room, still-room and maltings.

Outside the town, following the Fiddich upstream, lies Chivas-owned Allt à Bhainne distillery, built in 1975 to supply the blending industry.

GLENFIDDICH

Scotland's answer to château-bottled, Glenfiddich is one of only a tiny handful of distilleries bottling their whisky on the premises where it was made and matured.

More people have drunk Glenfiddich in its distinctive triangular bottle than any other single malt whisky. Its produc-

tion is scaled to meet the enormous demand, with eleven wash stills, eighteen spirit stills and warehousing for more than 250,000 maturing casks.

Glenfiddich's lightly peated, gentle character has been responsible for wooing countless blends drinkers to the delights of single malts. Many make the pilgrimage to Dufftown to one of the busiest visitor centers and tourist attractions in the industry.

THE BALVENIE

Glenfiddich's sister distillery next door is proof of how adjoining whiskies can differ in character. They share the same water, from the Robbie Dubh (*doo*) well, and the same malt supplies, yet remain mysteriously different.

William Grant built the distillery in 1892, largely from second-hand equipment and it displays wonderful ingenuity. Its eight stills are steam-heated by surplus heat piped from Glenfiddich next door.

In contrast to the seamless sophistication of Glenfiddich, The Balvenie – which takes its name from Balvenie Castle – was described by the late connoisseur Gordon Brown as "almost an Earl Grey tea mix of oily fruit and astringency."

CONVALMORE

One of the most dramatic sights in distilling history, worthy of a painting, was the October night in 1909 when Convalmore distillery caught fire in a snowstorm. Flames were said to have risen thirty feet (9 metres), engulfing most of the buildings and their equipment.

Convalmore rose from the ashes to face a chequered future of takeovers and mothballing, and has not produced whisky for some years. The malt, which is available from independent bottlers Gordon & MacPhail, is quite robust, unusual and worth sampling.

THE BALVENIE

Owner:	William Grant & Sons
Age:	10 years; 40%
Color:	Deep gold
Aroma:	Full and aromatic with fruit and honey.
Taste:	Full-bodied, rounded flavor. A slight dryness giving way to honey sweetness in the finish.
Comment:	Bold and rich in character; a fine after-dinner malt.

CONVALMORE

Owner:	United Distillers
Age:	1969 (Gordon & MacPhail bottling); 40%
Color:	Pale amber
Aroma:	A delicate, rather sweet nose. John Lamond described it as having "the smell of a cornfield after rain in summer."
Taste:	Medium-sweet with a smooth mouth-feel. A pleasant peaty dryness slipping into a spicy, gingerbread finish.
Comment:	A seldom-sung whisky with the girth required for after-dinner drinking. Worth exploring.

The Dufftown Circle

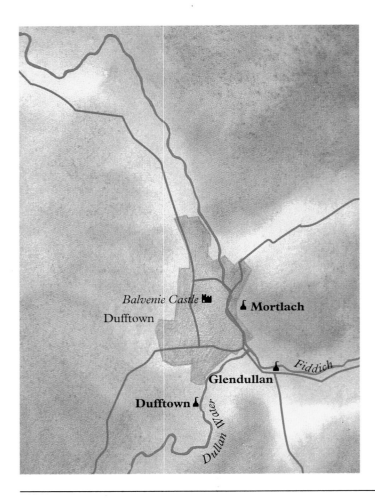

This little corner of Speyside covers a small area, but Dufftown has enormous stature as an ancient center of distilling. The town lies at the intersection of the fertile glens of the Fiddich and the Dullan. While Glenfiddich and The Balvenie overshadow everything around here, the semi-circle of Dufftown, Mortlach and Glebdullan respond with almost a local style of their own – bold, well-rounded malts, rich without being too heavy; and with surprising depths.

DUFFTOWN (*duff-ton*)

Dufftown-Glenlivet distillery nestles in Dullan Glen, overlooked by ridges of saw-tooth pines and surrounded by the rising smoke of other distilleries.

It was founded in 1896 by two Liverpool businessmen, Peter MacKenzie and Richard Stackpole, who were bent on making their own Speyside whisky. The distillery, built from local stone, soon acquired a reputation based to a great extent on the water it drew from Jock's Well. It was so pure that several attempts were made by nearby Mortlach distillery to divert the burn and hijack supplies.

Dufftown, which can barely claim to be a Glenlivet, produces whisky good enough in its own right not to require the borrowed appellation. Much of its output goes to Bells for blending, and demand is so high that a sister distillery, Pittyvaich, was built with carefully duplicated stills in an attempt to boost production without putting Dufftown's well-balanced flavor at risk.

MORTLACH

Mortlach took out a licence in 1824 and had the distinction of being the first of Dufftown's original seven legal distilleries. Because of this, and its whisky, it has always been regarded with some veneration locally.

For a time, in the early 1920s, it was the biggest distillery

DUFFTOWN

Owner:	United Distillers
Age:	10 years; 40%
Color:	Light amber
Aroma:	Light and slightly floral with subdued peat smoke.
Taste:	Smooth, medium-bodied with a touch of dryness.
Comment:	Dufftown is an honest workaday whisky used for blending in Bells. Worth trying as an anytime dram, but largely undistinguished.

Above: Dufftown-Glenlivet distillery nestles in the woodland of Dullan Glen outside the town in a scene which could be half a century ago.

In some fundamentalist corners of the Highlands, the Kirk eyed whisky-making with unease. Mortlach appears to have been an exception – when it lay silent for a while, the granary was turned into a chapel.

Mostly, it has been bottled by independents, though owners United Distillers bottle a 16 years old. With its characteristic fruity smoothness, Mortlach deserves a wider audience.

GLENDULLAN

Despite hiding its light under a bushel, this greatly overlooked malt has some distinguished supporters. King Edward VII developed a taste for it in 1902. In recent years the distillery produces an outstanding "own name" single malt for the Houses of Parliament in London.

Madam Speaker's Order, chosen by Betty Boothroyd the Speaker of the House at a tasting in the Westminster cellars, shares a light, dry nose with Glendullan's other malts. The first 3,000 bottles of Madam Speaker's Order were delivered in presentation boxes to the House of Commons at the end of 1995 and sold out within days. Demand was probably based more on the twenty-pound bargain price and exclusivity than the mild malt's modest character. Madame Speaker's Ordercarries no age statement but, like the lady herself, exhibits a sweetness concealing a smooth intensity.

When Glendullan was built in 1897, both its water source and the proximity of the railway determined the site. The distillery shared a private railway siding with nearby Mortlach on the Great North of Scotland Railway.

For many years the distillery was powered by water from the Fiddich and was only connected to the national electricity grid after World War II. An additional distillery was built in 1972 to increase capacity and in 1975 replaced the old plant.

Glendullan is an essential contributor to Old Parr, the most popular de luxe blend in Japan.

in the area. Mortlach's water, flowing from the Conval Hills, attracted an illicit still to the site in the eighteenth century. It is quite distinctive, producing a fine whisky, which makes it all the more puzzling why once they coveted Dufftown's supply.

MORTLACH

Owner:	United Distillers
Age:	12 years; 40%
Color:	Yellow-gold
Aroma:	Well-composed aroma of some depth. Initial malty smokiness gives way to intriguing notes of fruit and spices.
Taste:	Bold and full-bodied. A very mellow malt with pleasant fruitiness.
Comment:	Well-rounded and worth revisiting.

GLENDULLAN

Owner:	United Distillers
Age:	12 years; 43%
Color:	Lemon-gold
Aroma:	Aromatic – apples and fruit with a hint of sherry.
Taste:	Bold-flavored, mellow-bodied and clean on the palate with a warming finish.
Comment:	Often overlooked and deserving of more credit than it receives. A pleasant after-dinner malt.

An Elegant Trio: Cardhu, Tamdhu & Knockando

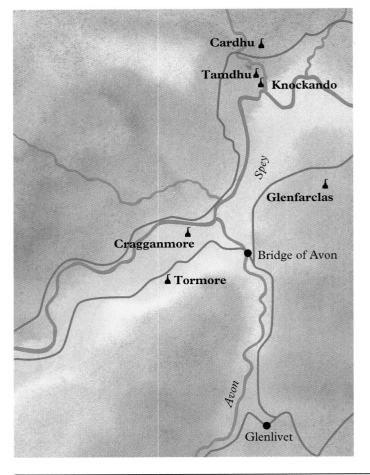

This small distilling community on the northwest bank of the Upper Spey shares a light, soft style which attracts increasing attention, particularly from those keen to explore single malts for the first time.

CARDHU (car-doo)

The distillery lies on the site of an old illicit still in salmon fishing country, commanding spectacular views across the Craigallachie Valley and providing an excellent vantage point to spot approaching excisemen.

Cardhu began as a distilling farm, taking its soft spring water and peat from nearby Mannoch Hill. It still maintains a fifteen-acre (6ha) farm producing barley, sheep and cattle.

Helen Cumming, the original farmer's wife, provided accommodation for visiting gaugers. When they were in residence, she hoisted a red flag over her barn to warn local distillers to hide their equipment.

For generations, the Cummings were hard-working Highlanders, making whisky by hand long after distilleries around them had modernized. Alfred Barnard described the buildings as "of the most struggling and primitive description and, although water power existed, a great part of the work was done by manual labor. It is wonderful," he reflected, "how long this state of things existed, considering the successful business that was carried on for so many years."

Cardhu was so proud of its single malt that its advertizing boldly proclaimed it to be the only Speyside distillery not to attach "Glenlivet" to its name. Cardhu makes a significant contribution to Johnnie Walker blends.

TAMDHU (tam-doo)

Tamdhu distillery is set in thick woodland around the Victorian railway station of Knockando, which now comprises the visitors' center.

CARDHU

Owner:	United Distillers
Age:	12 years; 40%
Color:	Pale
Aroma:	A lightly aromatic nose with delicate whiffs of fruit.
Taste:	Sweet and mellow with nicely balanced peatiness and a long finish.
Comment:	A pleasant way to broach the acquaintance of single malts.

TAMDHU

Owner:	Highland Distilleries
Age:	10 years; 40%
Color:	Pale gold
Aroma:	Clean and fresh with a crisp, biscuity nose and faint hint of smoke.
Taste:	Lightly rounded with a distinct touch of toffee.
Comment:	Widely available and right for most occasions.

ESTABLISHED 1897
TAMDHU
SPEYSIDE SCOTLAND

Above: Cardhu distillery's perfumed whisky, bottled as a single malt since the 1960s, is a major contributor to Johnnie Walker Gold Label.

Right: Light, fragrant Knockando 1982. The age of each bottle is declared so that devotees may detect nuances from one season to the next.

Tamdhu's light, smoky whisky is a curiosity in that it emerges from probably the last distillery to use Saladin Boxes for malting barley. The method, which was named after French engineer Charles Saladin, replaced the traditional malting floor in some distilleries. Barley is tipped into ten shallow troughs through which warm air is blown while metal forks travel back and forth turning the grain. Germination is stopped by kilning over peat smoke in the usual way.

Tamdhu, which has a pleasant, almost toasty flavor, is a component of Famous Grouse blend.

KNOCKANDO

Knockando has an interesting approach to whisky, releasing it when it is considered at its peak rather than at a predetermined age. This means that every single bottle of Knockando is vintage, carrying a specific year on the label.

While each season is evaluated for its readiness, Knockando is generally judged to have reached perfection between twelve and fifteen years old. There are exceptions – occasionally, when a few casks stand out, they are held back to mature longer (twenty to twenty-five years is not uncommon) and released in limited quantities.

The distillery acknowledges the contribution made by sherry casks, but limits use of them to avoid dominating the flavor. The result is a delicate, finely balanced malt which rightly earns a seat in the Speyside Valhalla.

Knockando (which means the "little black hill" in Gaelic) sits on a steep wooded bank of the river, where it holds the sole rights to the water from Cardnach Spring. The whisky claims to owe its special delicacy and fragrance to the purity of this spring water.

KNOCKANDO

Owner:	Justerini & Brooks
Age:	1982; 43%; plain wood matured.
Color:	Pale honey
Aroma:	Light and honey-sweet with faint smokiness.
Taste:	A clean smooth body with vanilla sweetness.
Comment:	When matured in a fifty-fifty mix of plain and sherrywood, the 1982 sports a rich sherry aroma and has a creamy mouth-feel.

The Upper Reaches of the Spey

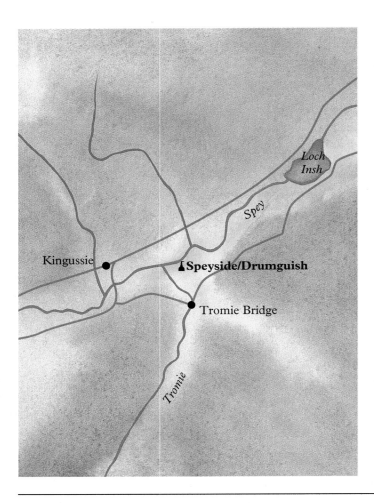

Speyside distillery lies so far up the Spey that it is almost in the Central Highlands. It is not only the smallest on Speyside but also the newest; so new, in fact, that a malt bearing the label is not yet ready. Enthusiasts have had to make do with a full-bodied vanilla-and-almonds 3 Years Old called Drumguish. The distillery started production in 1989 and draws its water from the River Tromie less than a mile before it enters the Spey.

Traveling downstream from Grantown-on-Spey the first sight of a distillery in the world's most famous whisky heartland comes as a surprise. Tormore, dominating the main road amid the hills, resembles a Bavarian railway station.

The first Highland distillery to be built this century was designed in 1958 by Sir Albert Richardson, past President of the Royal Academy of Art in London, and, to his credit, line and form blend beautifully with the surrounding countryside.

The Upper Spey, from Tormore to where it is joined by the Fiddich at Cragganmore, has attracted an assembly of distilleries producing whisky of wonderful individuality, smoothness and complexity such as Cragganmore, Knockando, Glenfarclas and Aberlour.

This elite circle is dominated by the great rock plug of Ben Rinnes (2,759ft/841m), Speyside's most celebrated mountain and one from which a variety of burns, springs and wells originate. Ben Rinnes granite, a molten intrusion created millions of years ago, is the source of fine hill water used by no less than eleven distilleries.

TORMORE (see map on page 46)
Tormore distillery manages to combine architectural elegance with tradition – even its bottle label and packaging are mod-

---

TORMORE

Owner:	Allied Domecq
Age:	10 years; 43%
Color:	Full-gold
Aroma:	Soft and rounded with a honeyed sweetness.
Taste:	A silky body with all the well-balanced, lightly sweet characteristics of a great Speyside malt.
Comment:	Extremely palatable.

CRAGGANMORE

Owner:	United Distillers
Age:	12 years; 40%
Color:	Amber
Aroma:	Drier than many Speyside malts, with great depth. Michael Jackson declared it, "the most complex aroma of any malt".
Taste:	A firm body with pleasant herbal notes and a malty, smooth finish.
Comment:	An excellent malt to select for a tasting session – sure to elicit a wide variety of impressions.

ern – but one of its real assets is its water.

Achvochkie Burn, a tributary of the Spey, flows off surrounding moorland, through granite, to surface icy cold and exceptionally pure.

Tormore is aged for ten years to produce a mellow, delicate, well-rounded whisky. Its smoothness makes it a good entry-level malt, a fact not overlooked by marketeers who pitch it directly at twenty-somethings.

CRAGGANMORE (see map on page 46)
An impressive pedigree of distilling excellence lay behind Cragganmore when it opened in 1869. Founder John Smith had managed The Macallan, launched the new Glenlivet distillery ten years earlier and leased nearby Glenfarclas.

Cragganmore is famous for being the first distillery to use rail transport and built a small private siding to accommodate the "Whisky Express", which is proudly featured on the label.

Smith, a huge man of twenty-two stone (140kg) was particularly fond of the train because it was virtually the only way he could get around – even though he was obliged to travel in the guard's van because the carriage doors were too narrow.

Before carefully designing his distillery, which is laid out in a quadrangle, Smith spent some time analyzing water from the local burn, which is fed by springs from nearby Craggan More hill. Only when it met his satisfaction were foundations laid.

GLENFARCLAS (see map on page 46)
Glenfarclas, which means "glen of the green grassland" in Gaelic, sits on the slopes of Ben Rinnes near the junction of the Avon and the Spey.

When it was built in 1836, the distillery malted its own barley with local peat, a tradition which continued until the 1970s. Glenfarclas began life as a farm distillery and has remained in the ownership of the John and George Grant fam-

ily, who still keep a herd of Aberdeen Angus cattle.

Glenfarclas "105" is a robust, assertive malt which, at 60 per cent proof is not only serious stuff but probably the strongest distillery-bottled single malt. It is known affectionately as "The 105" after its classification under the old proofing system. One sip sends the message that this malt is not to be treated lightly.

Above left: Drumguish - the first expression from Speyside distillery, the smallest, newest and most difficult to find of the region's many producers.

Below: Tormore is one of Speyside's most imposing distilleries. Its very drinkable whisky, available as a 10 Years Old, is equally pleasing.

GLENFARCLAS

Owner:	J & G Grant
Age:	10 years; 40%
Color:	Straw-gold highlights
Aroma:	Delicately sweet and leafy with a coffee tang.
Taste:	Malty sweet; full, rich and round with a slightly spicy finish.
Comment:	Deep and characterful. Ideal for the end of an evening.

A Mountain Gathering: Benrinnes, Glenallachie & Aberlour

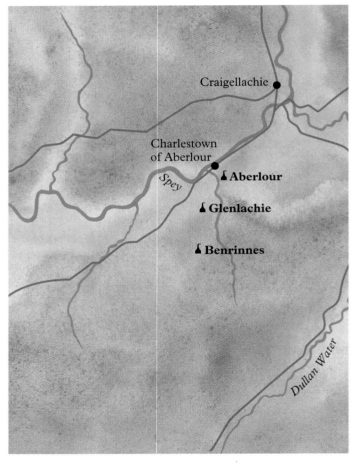

This trio of Upper Spey distilleries huddles beneath the imposing bulk of Ben Rinnes for which they depend on their water. Supplies from deep granite springs and snow-fed burns give local whiskies a clean, light freshness.

BENRINNES (ben-rin-is)

Ben Rinnes mountain, which commands a view of nine counties, is a landmark for fishermen on the Moray Firth. In 1887, Alfred Barnard wrote that water flowing from its upper reaches to Benrinnes distillery "can be seen on a clear day some miles distant, sparkling over the prominent rocks on its downward course, passing over mossy banks and gravel, which perfectly filters it."

Benrinnes single malt has another distinction in using a form of triple-distillation. Stills are grouped in threes, rather than the customary wash-still/spirit-still pairing and the new spirit comes off slightly stronger at around 76 per cent.

The original distillery was swept away when the Spey spectacularly burst its banks in 1829, causing widespread damage. The new building then gave sixty years service before being destroyed by fire in 1899. The present premises have happily managed to avoid the biblical fate of destruction by pestilence.

Its position on the slopes of Ben Rinnes took advantage of outstanding mountain water but had the disadvantage of remoteness; for many years supplies of barley had to be brought to the distillery by horse and cart from Aberlour station three miles away.

Ben Rinnes can be found in a 1969 vintage from specialist merchants, a version admired for its creamy liqueur qualities.

GLENALLACHIE (glen-aleck-y)

These days, Glenallachie is used almost exclusively in House of Campbell blends, such as Clan Campbell. It deserves resurrecting as a self and once appeared as such under a previous

---

BENRINNES

Owner:	United Distillers
Age:	15 years; 43%
Color:	Deep straw with gold highlights
Aroma:	Lightly peated with rounded fruitiness.
Taste:	Dry, firm and biscuity with a sweetish finish.
Comment:	Lacking the restorative qualities of an aperitif, but light and dry enough for pre-dinner drinking.

GLENALLACHIE

Owner:	House of Campbell (Pernod Ricard)
Age:	12 years; 40%
Color:	Pale straw
Aroma:	Fresh and delicate; quite sweet.
Taste:	Clean-tasting and surprisingly full, with a smooth, sweet finish.
Comment:	Unexpectedly complex and worth seeking out in independent bottling.

into the top ten malts worldwide.

The distillery, on the steep banks of the Spey, on the outskirts of rose-clad Charleston-of-Aberlour, draws water from St. Dunstan's Well, named after a former Archbishop of Canterbury who settled nearby here on a mission to convert the Highlands.

Aberlour has several idiosyncrasies which possibly contribute to its flavor: among them an insistence on using Scottish barley, usually from the Black Isle, and casking with cork bungs (as opposed to wood) in the belief that they allow harsher, unwanted elements to escape. It is matured partly in sherry casks, which are hand-picked each year in Jerez, and which contribute beautifully to the flavor.

The distillery has had its share of drama. It was destroyed by fire in 1879, but villagers rolled out the barrels and saved the whisky. A century later, the well dried-up but miraculously sprang to life again the day Aberlour won the International Wine & Spirit Competition gold medal.

incarnation. It is still available in limited quantities from independent bottlers.

Comparatively modern, Glenallachie was built in 1968 but closed in 1987 after a change of ownership. It was later sold to the French drinks giant Pernod Ricard, proprietors of neighboring Aberlour, and is now back in production.

There is a consensus that Glenallachie would be well-received if marketed again. "Greatly underrated" and "deserves a greater reputation" figure among favorable comments.

ABERLOUR

One of the outstanding Speyside malts on the market. Sales in the past decade have been meteoric, deservedly propelling it

---

ABERLOUR

Owner:	House of Campbell (Pernod Ricard)
Age:	12 years; 43%
Color:	Ruby-amber
Aroma:	Full and rounded with delightful notes of mint and Highland toffee.
Taste:	Let the Aberlour Flavour Wheel speak for itself: rich, vanilla and sherried with honey, chocolate, sweetoak, toffee and mint.
Comment:	One of a handful of malts like nectar when tasted neat.

Imperial, Dailuaine & Craigellachie

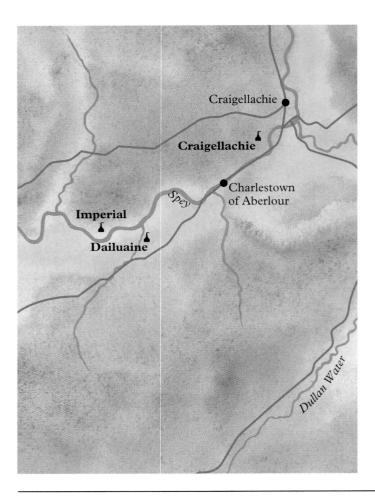

The last three distilleries of the Upper Spey: neighboring Imperial and Dailuaine are home to two robust, yet very different malts while, at the meeting of the Fiddich and the Spey, we discover the smoky pungency of Craigellachie.

Geographers would classify this definition of the Upper Spey as actually the lower course of the river. The true upper reaches lie many miles to the southwest. But as whisky drinkers lose interest when there are no distilleries in sight it is perhaps wiser to ignore the constraints of cartography and simply follow our noses.

IMPERIAL

Imperial was built in 1897, the year of Queen Victoria's Diamond Jubilee, and the distillery was topped with a gilded crown to honor the occasion.

Half a century later, the device rusted and had to be dismantled. It was the inspiration of Speyside architect Charles Doig, who was responsible for designing many famous distilleries and – as legend has it – the distinctive pagoda chimneys that top them.

Imperial, in the tiny village of Carron on the banks of the Spey, has four stills producing 500,000 gallons (2,273,000 litres/600,000 US gallons) a year and is not widely bottled.

The distillery has suffered an unfortunate history. Two years after opening, it closed in the 1899 whisky slump and remained padlocked for twenty years. It closed again in a 1925 ownership change and hardly produced any more whisky until it was rebuilt thirty years later.

Although it is seldom seen, Imperial is worth searching for. This is one of the gracious old ladies of the Spey.

DAILUAINE (dall-you-an)

The "Green Vale" distillery, as it translates from the Gaelic, lies a mile (1.6km) along the road from Imperial. At the turn

---

IMPERIAL

Owner:	Allied Domecq
Age:	1970; 40% (Gordon & MacPhail bottling)
Color:	Deep gold
Aroma:	Rich and restrained; slightly perfumed and sweet.
Taste:	Bold and full with peat, heather and deep autumnal notes.
Comment:	Great Speyside sipping whisky for curling up with a good book.

DAILUAINE

Owner:	United Distillers
Age:	16 years; 43%
Color:	Pale amber
Aroma:	Dry and fairly smoky with a peppery background.
Taste:	Robust, fruity and sweet with the pepper turning to a touch of spice.
Comment:	Try it with a slice of fruit cake.

Dailuaine has produced its full-bodied, fruity malt since 1852, much of which goes into Johnnie Walker.

CRAIGELLACHIE (*kray-gell-achy*)

There's no mistaking the main destination of Craigellachie: the name of White Horse Distillers is emblazoned above the tall windows of the still room.

Below the distillery's perch on the Rock of Craigellachie, the River Spey winds under Telford's elegant 1815 single-span iron bridge.

Despite its setting, Craigellachie was seldom a haven of tranquillity under the chairmanship of White Horse founder Sir Peter Mackie, known to his staff as "restless Peter".

Before his death in 1924, he decided to move 2,300 casks of Craigellachie whisky to Campbeltown, on the other side of Scotland. The operation involved running chartered trains for four days from Craigellachie Junction to the port of Lossiemouth, where casks were loaded onto two freighters which then sailed around the northern tip of Scotland to the Mull of Kintyre.

Other business enthusiasms of Sir Peter Mackie's included making BBM (Bran, Bone & Muscle), a patented flour which all staff were obliged to use at home; animal feed cakes; concrete panelling; Highland tweed; and Carrageen moss, which was used for making blancmange. Without exception, these projects were relinquished with relief at his passing. The refreshing pungency of Craigellachie mirrored his character and fortunately lives on.

Above: Telford's single-span bridge near Craigellachie distillery. The fine whisky produced here is one of the most underrated in the region.

Below right: Dailuaine distillery today. The original, destroyed in a fire in 1917, had the first pagoda roof in the industry.

of the century the two were jointly owned, but have since gone their separate ways.

Change did not always come rapidly to the Highlands. It was 1950 before Dailuaine was connected to the national electricity grid. Alternative power, in the form of two Heath Robinson water wheels, was still on standby in the 1960s.

For more than a hundred years the familiar plume of steam from the daily "puggie" – the workhorse locomotive of the Highland railway – rose above the trees. The "Dailuaine No.1" gleamed with paint and polished brass as it delivered coal and barley and departed creaking under casks of whisky.

CRAIGELLACHIE

Owner:	United Distillers
Age:	14 years; 43%
Color:	Lemon straw
Aroma:	Sweet and pungent with a light touch of peat smoke.
Taste:	Smooth with a light smokiness and a long finish.
Comment:	Light enough to follow a lengthy dinner.

Malts of the Lower Spey

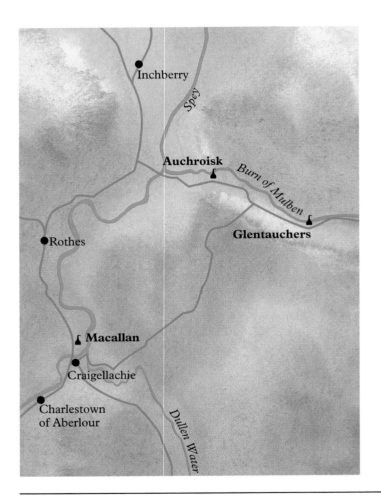

From the home of the mighty Macallan in the Craigellachie Valley, the Spey ambles broadly through woods and fields towards the distant steam rising from the distillery town of Rothes. Beyond lie two distilleries of quiet distinction: the Singleton of Auchroisk and seldom-seen Glentauchers.

THE MACALLAN

For most of its 173-year history, the single malt whisky from this distillery was known simply as Macallan and seldom advertized. As late as the 1960s it was still available only locally, and it largely remained so until a concerted marketing campaign in the 1980s added the definite article and propelled it into the world sales league.

The distillery lies near a ford across the Spey on an ancient cattle route typical of the unmapped roads favored by smugglers. Indeed, it is believed that distilling has been carried out at Macallan since the 1700s.

Demands from blenders for its exquisitely smooth, sherry-sweet single malt led to expansion in the 1950s. The proprietors wisely stuck to small stills, rather than installing huge versions, in the belief that the quality of the whisky would thus be maintained.

In the 1960s, output was doubled by building what amounted to a second distillery. To avoid any drift in quality, the new spirit was allowed to stand in glass-lined tanks before it was casked.

The distillery is famous for its adherence to sherry casks and takes steps to secure supplies. New casks are commissioned and shipped to Scotland after two or three years use in Jerez. Thanks in part to such meticulous cask management,

---

THE MACALLAN

Owner: The Macallan-Glenlivet plc

Age: 10 years; 40%

Color: Rich amber-gold

Aroma: Its reputation rushes to greet you with rich, velvety notes of sherry, almonds, pears and heather.

Taste: Full and smooth in the mouth with voluptuous character. A touch of sherry and wood and a lingering aftertaste.

Comment: One of the least peaty of all single malts. A classic example of the art and craft of whisky making.

THE SINGLETON OF AUCHROISK

Owner: Justerini & Brooks

Age: 10 years; 40%

Color: Old gold

Aroma: Medium-sweet with nicely balanced sherry notes.

Taste: Smooth mouth-feel and a flavor of nuts. Unexpectedly short finish leaves a faint taste of cloves.

Comment: Makes up in sophistication what it lacks in personality. A pleasant after-dinner malt.

Left: The Macallan, at the richer, fuller end of the Speyside spectrum, is the only single malt matured exclusively in sherrywood.

probably matched only by Glenmorangie, The Macallan is a malt of tremendous finesse with rare softness and grace.

THE SINGLETON OF AUCHROISK (*oth-rusk*)

This is another malt whisky of sherried elegance, though comparatively new. The name, like the whisky, is quite a mouthful. Presumably, it prompted the proprietors to solve the pronunciation problem by calling it The Singleton (i.e. singular malt) of Auchroisk.

Curiously, they hit on something. A marketing survey has shown that many professional men in their thirties would like to develop a taste for single malts but are afraid to ask for them for fear of pronouncing the name incorrectly.

Although the Singleton is fairly new to this stretch of the Spey, it has, nevertheless, collected fifteen major international awards in ten years.

Its meticulously neat buildings were laid out in 1975 on the site of an ancient spring, Dorie's Well. The source of soft water said to form the basis of the whisky's mellow character.

Above: The clean lines of Auchroisk distillery, which produces an equally clean-tasting malt. Unusually, the entire output is bottled.

Below: Sales of the Macallan have been boosted by its witty advertising, mostly the work of director and scriptwriter Alan Shiach.

Its gentle, sherried style is aimed directly at blended drinkers interested in moving on to a single malt.

GLENTAUCHERS (*glen-tockers*)

These days, the entire output of Glentauchers goes for blending and expressions can be found only in merchants' bottlings. The distillery, in the hamlet of Mulben, was opened in 1987 and originally owned by whisky baron James Buchanan, founder of Black & White. Under his direction, experiments were carried out to distil malt whisky by a continuous method, but these plans were abandoned.

Glentauchers has six stills, producing 440,000 gallons (2,000,000 litres/528,000 US gallons) a year, and draws its water from the Rosarie Burn.

GLENTAUCHERS

Owner:	Allied Domecq
Age:	1979; 40% (Gordon & MacPhail bottling)
Color:	Pale amber
Aroma:	Rich with pear drop touches and honeysuckle fragrance.
Taste:	Light with fresh, estery influences and a nice dry finish.
Comment:	Aperitif standard.

Nature's Garden: Speyburn & Glen Grant

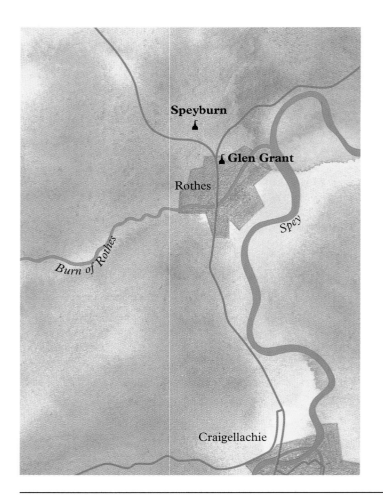

In 1829, the tiny but important distilling town of Rothes was almost destroyed when the Spey burst its banks. Upstream, Benrinnes distillery was swept away in the same disaster. Crowds gathered from miles to witness the scene.

Today, Rothes has no shortage of attractions: arboriculturists are drawn to heavily planted forests at Rosarie and Teindland, while the pull for whisky lovers is the town's five distilleries. Two whisky producers offer arboreal attractions of their own: legendary Glen Grant with its splendidly restored Victorian garden and Speyburn in what is perhaps the most idyllic setting of all Highland distilleries.

SPEYBURN

All the romance in the world cannot disguise the fact that distilleries are factories for making whisky. Try as they may, few could hope to aspire to the shortbread-tin status of Speyburn, set in breathtaking countryside.

The distillery is a handsome Victorian building with its pagoda protruding above the trees in a thickly wooded fold of hills in the Glen of Rothes. It was opened in 1897, with the idea of production commencing on 1 November so that the the first fillings would be able to bear the date of Queen Victoria's Diamond Jubilee.

Anyone who has experienced problems with builders will understand the directors' chagrin. Production finally started in the last week in December and the stillhouse had no windows fitted. A blizzard blasted through, forcing staff to work in overcoats. Despite their valiant efforts, by the chime of midnight at New Year, only one butt had been bonded with the crucial date on its head.

Speyburn's architect was Charles Doig from Elgin, ten miles (16km) away, who was to distillery design what Frank Matcham was to theaters. One feature Doig didn't plan was Speyburn's resident ghost, who has made his presence known

SPEYBURN

Owners:	Inver House Distillers
Age:	10 years; 40%
Color:	Copper
Aroma:	Dry and fresh with heather honey notes.
Taste:	Big, full-bodied and malty with a long, sweet finish.
Comment:	A smooth, satisfying after-dinner malt.

to the night shift. The distillery was built on the site of Rothes' gibbet, which was formerly the site of execution for local criminals and cattle rustlers.

Speyburn, with its profound malty sweet aroma, was the first single malt distillery to install drum-maltings, quite literally a revolutionary development in which barley is placed in large rotating drums and the temperature controlled by blasts of air.

GLEN GRANT

One of the world's most popular single malt whiskies began life on a Rothes farm which had been run by the Grant brothers, John and James, for six years before they decided to turn their surplus crops to whisky distilling.

One of the galvanizing factors was water from crystal-clear Caperdonich Spring in the hillside above the distillery. Glen Grant, distinctively light in color with a smooth, clean taste, had tremendous appeal for whisky drinkers and climbed to become the second biggest seller worldwide.

John's nephew, Major James Grant, took over in 1872 at the age of twenty-five and guided the distillery's fortunes for sixty years. One of his greatest achievements, apart from making memorable whisky, was to lay out the beautiful gardens behind the distillery.

Above: The whisky safe installed by Major Grant in his distillery garden. Here he could pause to admire the view and pour himself a dram.

Right: Glen Grant, a single malt with a solid export pedigree. One of the first to be bottled and widely sold in Scotland at the turn of the century.

They formed a lush brush-stroke of fifty acres (20ha) of woodland, waterfalls, salmon pools, lily ponds, gorges, a burn and wild meadows. He loved to take dinner guests on a tour of his greenhouses, where he grew orchids, peaches, melons and grapes, followed by a tour of the gardens.

At the top of the garden he built a rustic bridge over a waterfall where the burn flows through a narrow ravine. Here, the Major installed a safe in the rock wall where he kept a bottle of Glen Grant and some glasses, with sparkling cold water from the burn for anyone who wished it.

The current owners, Chivas, have now restored the garden and, in 1996, it was opened to the public after three years effort by a dedicated team of craftsmen, tree surgeons, horticulturists and landscapers, working from Victorian Ordnance Survey maps to complete the project.

Like the whisky itself, there is something there for everyone. Glen Grant is a versatile malt which can be drunk on a range of occasions, with a distinctive label and packaging which has changed little since 1840.

GLEN GRANT

Owners:	Chivas Brothers
Age:	10 years; 43%
Color:	Pale straw
Aroma:	Light and fresh with creamy fruitiness and a subtle fragrance.
Taste:	Its famous dryness is balanced with distinctly fruity flavors and a hint of sweet nuttiness in the finish.
Comment:	One of the Speyside greats. Has been compared to its stablemate The Glenlivet for its elegant integration of peatiness and sweetness. Delightful before dinner.

The Reclusives of Rothes: Caperdonich, The Glen Rothes & Glen Spey

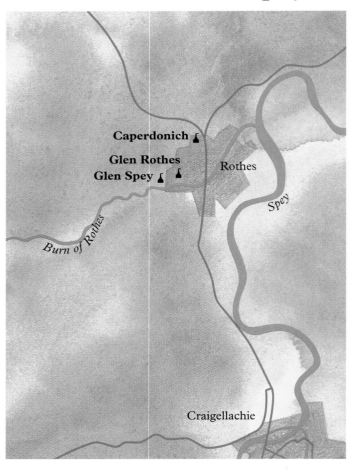

These three reclusive distilleries, huddled around Rothes, are the last on this final stretch of the Lower Spey before it cuts a broad course to the North Sea. Their malts are not widely available but, nevertheless, worth searching for. From here the whisky trail turns to follow the River Lossie as it flows northwest to the mouth of the Moray Firth.

CAPERDONICH

Major James Grant, the man who built the gardens of Glen Grant, turned his attention to building another distillery in 1897. Caperdonich, originally known as Glen Grant Number Two, was constructed across the road from Glen Grant. The two distilleries were joined by a pipe, prompting local Rothes' residents to boast that their streets "flowed with whisky".

In 1901, after the turn-of-the-century whisky slump, Caperdonich was padlocked and did not distill again until 1965, constituting one of the longest closures in distilling history. It was later rebuilt and renamed after Caperdonich Well which supplies Glen Grant's water.

Although it has always stood in the shadow of its more illustrious next of kin, Caperdonich's light, delicate whisky has enjoyed modest success in its own right. Demand led to two more stills being installed but, sadly, it remains unbottled by its owners.

THE GLEN ROTHES

One of the more richly nosed malts of the region. The water used by Glen Rothes, from the Burn of Rothes, is soft and tinged brown with peat from the Mannoch Hills and is ideally suited to whisky making.

The Glen Rothes, often talked of without the definite article, opened in 1987 and its stills were fired for the first time on the night of the storm that destroyed the Tay Rail Bridge (and almost wiped out Balmeneach distillery). The Great Tay

---

CAPERDONICH

Owner:	Seagram
Age:	1979; 40% (Gordon & MacPhail bottling)
Color:	Pale gold
Aroma:	Fragrant and sweet with faint touch of fruit.
Taste:	Lightly peated but not lacking in character. The finish fades rather quickly.
Comment:	One bottler (Cadenhead's) describes Caperdonich as "an abrasive whisky", but perhaps this credits it with more attack than it deserves.

THE GLEN ROTHES

Owner:	Highland Distilleries
Age:	8 Years Old; 40% (Gordon & MacPhail bottling)
Color:	Mid-amber
Aroma:	Quite full and slightly sherried with a light touch of peat.
Taste:	Round, smooth and pleasantly sweet with a substantial finish.
Comment:	After dinner.

CONNOISSEURS CHOICE

SINGLE SPEYSIDE MALT SCOTCH WHISKY

GLENROTHES
DISTILLERY

DISTILLED 1957 DISTILLED

GORDON & MACPHAIL

70cl 40%vol

Bridge Disaster, which stunned Victorian society, precipitating endless dramatic lithographs, temporarily brought local life to a halt. Seemingly, however, not at Glen Rothes, where production proceeded unabated.

In 1963 the number of stills was increased from four to six: the additions carefully crafted replicas of the originals. Glen Rothes is a beautifully sweet, warming whisky of character.

GLEN SPEY

For many years this hauntingly fragrant single malt has neither been bottled by the distillery nor released for merchant bottling. Fortunately, older versions are available: Cadenhead's, for example, stock a 15 Years Old.

The distillery takes its water from the Doonie Burn. Its original maturation warehouse was reputed to be an ornate affair with elaborate pillars supporting an arched roof. Unfortunately, however, the roof collapsed in 1892 under the weight of snow, its decorative appeal proving no replacement for its weak engineering.

Today Glen Spey's main function, along with its stable mate Knockando, is as an important contributor to J&B blends, and in the 1970s it stepped-up production for blending. A wider audience for its unusual and very drinkable whisky is overdue.

Left: Caperdonich distillery lies across the road from Glen Grant. Its output goes almost entirely into Chivas blends.

Below: The Great Tay Bridge Disaster which shocked Victorian society a few days after Christmas, 1879. (Illustrated London News).

GLEN SPEY

Owner:	Justerini & Brooks
Age:	8 Years Old; 40%
Color:	Pale gold
Aroma:	Delicate and spirity with a floral fragrance.
Taste:	Sweet and smooth with a grassy elegance and gentle finish.
Comment:	Difficult to find but worth the effort. Suitable for any occasion.

Malts of the Lossie

The River Lossie winds to the west of the Spey, emerging in the North Sea among the sand dunes of Lossiemouth, the fishing port and birthplace of Britain's first Labour Prime Minister, Ramsay MacDonald.

The Victorian elegance of Elgin, home of Gordon & MacPhail, the world's largest whisky merchants, is encircled by the river. Elgin is also a prominent distilling location, producing brands which may not have achieved world status but which, nevertheless, remain whiskies of distinction.

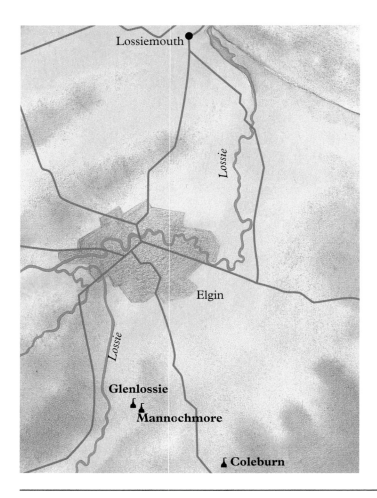

COLEBURN

Coleburn, which lies mid-way between Elgin and the neighboring distilling center of Rothes, is found mainly in independent bottlings.

Like many Highland distilleries, it lies close to those two essential components of whisky making: good water and a reliable railway. In Coleburn's case, it also had the advantage of a good architect: the noted Charles Doig, based four miles (6km) away in Elgin, who built the distillery from Moray sandstone with a blue roof of Welsh slate.

The original owner, John Robertson, described it in 1896 as "faced on one side by a plantation of Scotch firs and birches and swept by the cool mountain breezes of Brown Muir".

Sadly, the distillery closed in 1985, but its smooth, delicate whisky can be obtained fairly easily from merchants.

MANNOCHMORE

There is a long-running controversy about whether Mannochmore ever bottled its own whisky as a self. Cadenhead's certainly sell an 18 Years Old and the Scotch Malt Whisky Society has also bottled it.

Either way, Mannochmore has been available as a single malt only since 1992. The distillery, built in 1971, also produces Loch Dhu, the first black single malt, which claims to

---

COLEBURN

Owner:	United Distillers
Age:	1972; 40% (Gordon & MacPhail bottling)
Color:	Pale amber
Aroma:	Fresh and flowery with a pronounced peatiness.
Taste:	Dry and smooth; nicely balanced with a touch of sweetness.
Comment:	Refreshing, with an aperitif quality.

MANNOCHMORE

Owner:	United Distillers
Age:	12 Years Old; 43%
Color:	Pale straw
Aroma:	Lightly peated with slight fruitiness.
Taste:	Clean and quite dry.

Left: Glen Lossie distillery's elegant malting house and chimney by Charles Doig borrows heavily from his first pagoda-topped kiln at Dailuaine.

acquire its color from a process called "sweet double charring" and extended maturation; a curious companion for a malt almost the color of white wine. Whatever Loch Dhu's fortunes, it tastes delicious when generously sloshed into Christmas cake mixture.

GLEN LOSSIE

The distillery, which is situated in an area teeming with wildlife, features a long-eared owl and a greater spotted woodpecker on its labels.

Glen Lossie was designed by a publican, John Duff of the Fife Arms, Lhanbryde, who dreamed of owning his own distillery. His ingenious plans took advantage of the sloping site to use gravity "to render Glen Lossie independent of steam power". A seventy-foot (21m) drop from the distillery dam drove a waterwheel which powered machinery.

Glen Lossie gives pride of place to its horse-drawn fire engine, built in 1862, and employed to contain a fire which swept the buildings in 1929, causing the distillery £6,000 worth of damage.

Glen Lossie's twin, Mannochmore, is situated alongside. While they share the same process water and cooling water, they operate as separate distilleries, producing two entirely different whiskies.

LOCH DHU

Age:	10 Years Old; 40%
Color:	Velvety black
Aroma:	Strong touch of mint toffee
Taste:	Light and smooth with warming, spicy flavors.

GLEN LOSSIE

Owner:	United Distillers
Age:	10 Years Old; 43%
Color:	Pale gold
Aroma:	Clean and gently aromatic with a touch of heather.
Taste:	Smooth and soft on the palate with a lengthy, soothing finish.
Comment:	Mainly available through independents.

Two Sets of Twins

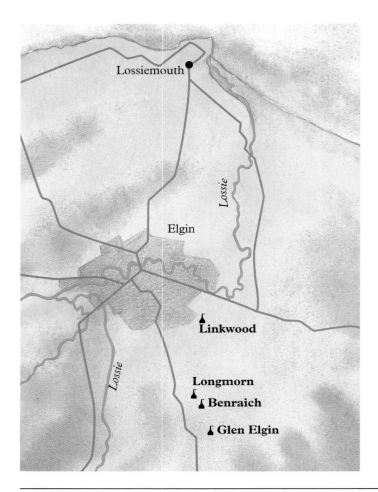

GLEN ELGIN

Building work on Glen Elgin began in 1898, just a few months before the terrible shadow of recession fell across the whisky industry. It was the last distillery to be built on Speyside for half a century; the next was Tormore in 1958.

Until 1950, Glen Elgin was lit and almost entirely operated by paraffin, and required a full-time trimmer to keep the lamps in order. Rebuilding in the 1960s gave the distillery a new lease of life and production happily trebled. It now produces around 440,000 gallons (2,000,000 litres/528,000 US gallons) of malt whisky a year, mainly for White Horse blend.

Glen Elgin is not to be confused with Gordon & MacPhail's vatted malt, Old Elgin.

BENRIACH

Benriach's pagodas are a prominent landmark on the main Elgin to Rothes road; the distillery's floor maltings, still in use, is one of only a handful left in the industry.

Benriach was built in 1898, a quarter of a mile from Longmorn, and named after nearby Riach Farm. Like its twin distillery, it draws its water from Burnside Springs.

Benriach closed for sixty-five years (in any other industry, mothballing plant for generations would be unthinkable) before surfacing again in 1965 to produce a soft malt with lightly balanced, fruity flavors in great demand for Seagram's blends.

LONGMORN

John Duff, one of the larger personalities of the Victorian whisky industry, built Longmorn and ploughed the profits into Benriach next door. Inspired by his success, he tried to set up similar ventures in South Africa and the United States but failed spectacularly.

Longmorn remained his finest achievement and enjoyed a high level of demand as a "top dressing" in many famous

---

GLEN ELGIN

Owner:	United Distillers
Age:	12 Years Old; 43%
Color:	Rich gold
Aroma:	Well-composed with heather-honey notes and light peating.
Taste:	Fresh and fruity with heather sweetness and a gentle finish.
Comment:	After-dinner malt.

BENRIACH

Owner:	Seagram
Age:	10 Years Old; 43% (distillery bottling)
Color:	Deep gold
Aroma:	Light: mellow softness enhanced by floral touches.
Taste:	Balanced, fruity flavors and delicate, dry finish.
Comment:	After years of availability only from independents, now relaunched as part of Seagram's heritage selection.

BENRIACH DISTILLERY
EST. 1898
A SINGLE
PURE HIGHLAND MALT
Scotch Whisky
Benriach Distillery, in the heart of the Highlands, still malts its own barley. The resulting whisky has a unique and attractive delicacy
PRODUCED AND BOTTLED BY THE
BENRIACH
DISTILLERY CO
ELGIN, MORAYSHIRE, SCOTLAND, IV30 3SJ
Distilled and Bottled in Scotland
AGED 10 YEARS
70cl e 43%vol

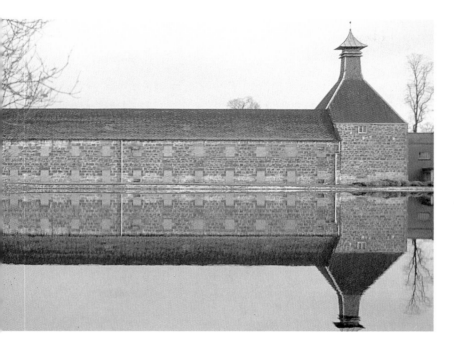

It has long been a favorite of merchants Gordon & MacPhail, who have bottled Linkwood for years and stock rare 1939 and 1946 vintages from the "silent" war years.

The distillery contributes to Bell's 8 Years Old and Johnnie Walker Black Label and is twinned with nearby Glen Elgin with which it shares a talented multi-skilled staff – the lady gardener also noses whisky as a member of the quality control team.

Above: One manager at Linkwood distillery used to so worry that changes would affect whisky quality that he left spiders' webs untouched.

Right: Benriach has been silent longer than it has been active in its 100-year history. Happily, it has now been recognized and re-released.

blends. In 1897 *The National Guardian* announced that it had "jumped into favour with buyers on the earliest day on which it was offered".

Longmorn has been described as "Speyside's best-kept secret". Its 15 Years Old is a cornerstone of Seagram's heritage selection.

LINKWOOD

This elegant Speyside malt with a fruity fragrance is produced close to Elgin. Originally a farm distillery, Linkwood pipes its water from springs near scenic Millbuies Loch.

LONGMORN

Owners:	Seagram
Age:	15 Years Old; 43%
Color:	Full gold
Aroma:	Full and rich with a delicate fragrance and gentle balance.
Taste:	Distinctive, floral flavors; rich, rounded mouth-feel; subtle, sweet finish.
Comment:	A revered malt of excellent quality.

LINKWOOD

Owner:	United Distillers
Age:	12 Years Old; 40%
Color:	Deep gold
Aroma:	Sherry-like qualities offset by subtle trace of peat smoke.
Taste:	Full and smooth with pleasantly rounded sweetness.
Comment:	Very stylish.

A Noble Trio

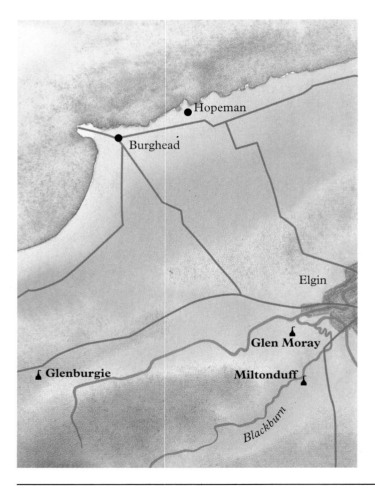

GLENBURGIE

For more than 180 years Glenburgie has nestled in a wooded valley surrounded by fertile Moray farmland, its soot-covered roofs barely visible from the main Aberdeen–Inverness road.

Alfred Barnard, visiting in 1887, described it as "a very ancient distillery, and about as old-fashioned as it is possible to conceive". Today, it still has the aura of a traditional distillery by-passed by progress.

It was founded by William Paul, grandfather of the distinguished nineteenth-century London surgeon, Dr. Liston Paul, and in the 1930s had the unusual, though not unique, distinction of a manageress in Miss Nichol.

Few distilleries have had women at the helm, the most notable being Laphroaig, where Bessie Williamson managed things in the 1950s and 1960s and, more recently, Glen Ord, which employs an unusually high proportion of female staff.

Miss Nicol guided the fortunes of Glenburgie with distinction. The whisky she presided over is largely unchanged, characterized by its distinctive sweetness and a spiciness reminiscent of Christmas cake.

MILTONDUFF

Legend has it that the waters of Miltonduff, the Black Burn, were blessed by the Abbot of nearby Pluscarden Abbey, famous locally for its fine ale. The benediction appears to have paid off for whisky makers – the burn supplied countless clandestine stills in the nineteenth century.

The distillery, established in 1824, has six pot stills, which are of identical size and shape to those installed more than a hundred years ago, to ensure continuity. It also retains links with agricultural origins by owning and managing several farms around the distillery.

Miltonduff is now one of the largest malt whisky distilleries in Scotland, capable of maintaining high production lev-

---

GLENBURGIE

Owner:	Allied Domecq
Age:	18 Years Old; 43%
Color:	Mid-amber.
Aroma:	Fresh with strong spicy, cinnamon notes.
Taste:	Very rich with touches of peat and a background of heather flowers.
Comment:	Pre-dinner or the perfect accompaniment to a winter meal.

MILTONDUFF

Owner:	Allied Domecq
Age:	12 Years Old; 43%
Color:	Clear soft gold
Aroma:	Fragrant. Flowery with hints of peat and vanilla, almonds and heather.
Taste:	Lightly peated with almond notes; delicately floral; touches of honey-sweetness.
Comment:	An after-dinner malt of great refinement.

Above: Milton Duff is a wonderful after-dinner malt, familiar in Japan, Europe and America, but deserving a wider UK audience.

Right: Glen Moray is a tribute to its elegant Georgian home-town of Elgin, the capital of Speyside whisky-making.

els of around 990,000 gallons (4,500,500 litres/1,188,000 US gallons) per annum.

GLEN MORAY

The historic old road to Elgin, which was traveled in the past by such figures as St. Columba, King Duncan and Bonnie Prince Charlie, passes through the distillery grounds.

GLEN MORAY

Owner:	MacDonald & Muir
Age:	12 Years Old; 40%
Color:	Pale amber
Aroma:	Light and fresh; slightly spicy and aromatic.
Taste:	Creamy mouth-feel with enjoyable notes of malt and heather.
Comment:	Has the potential of a mass market malt.

Glen Moray claims to be situated in a unique microclimate. The surrounding area, the Laich of Moray, is celebrated for its barley and extremely mild weather. An old weather saying asserts that "Moray has forty days more summer than any other part of Scotland".

For many years the distillery was a brewery using locally grown crops, but it converted to distilling in 1897. Glen Moray stands on the banks of the Lossie and its buildings are laid out around a central courtyard in the style of typical Highland farm buildings.

Despite the pleasant, light peatiness and rounded finish of its malt, in the distant past the distillery was forced to close due to shortage of demand. Since 1923, however, owners MacDonald & Muir of Glenmorangie have invested heavily, doubling capacity and vastly improving its fortunes.

65

Strathisla

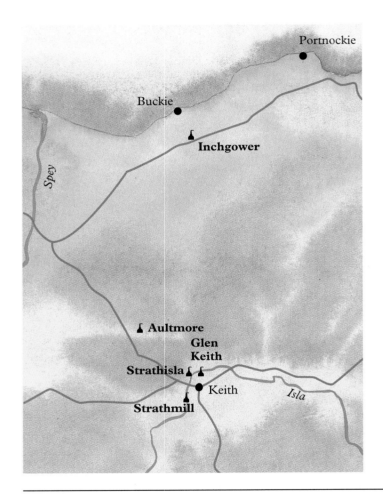

There are five distilleries strung along the *strath*, or valley, of the River Isla. Among them, Strathisla itself, which claims to be the oldest in the Highlands, and the sophisticated Glen Keith. Meanwhile, output from the J&B-owned Strathmill distillery is used exclusively for blending.

GLEN KEITH

A thought-provoking testament to the troubled years of malt whisky is the fact that Glen Keith, built in 1958, was the first distillery to open in Scotland this century.

It claimed another first in 1970 by installing a gas-fired still, a trend quickly adopted by many other whisky producers. Ten years later, Glen Keith attracted attention by introducing the first computer to control production.

Until quite recently, output was destined exclusively for Chivas Brothers (their fast-track Passport blend and 101 Pipers). Today, it is bottled as a single malt, or "self", in the Chivas Heritage Selection range.

Glen Keith was built on the site of an old meal mill on the banks of the River Isla, directly opposite its sister distillery Strathisla. It stands by the Linn of Keith, a picture postcard waterfall at the foot of what remains of the imposing six-foot-thick walls of Milton castle.

STRATHISLA

Originally known as Milton distillery, after the castle (see Glen Keith, above), Strathisla was founded in 1786. It was rebuilt a century later with a new kiln topped by two imposing pagoda vents and a water-wheel, making it one of the most idyllic distilleries in Scotland. The late whisky writer Gordon Brown aptly described the setting as "Hansel and Gretel".

Strathisla also claims to be one of the oldest distilleries in Scotland, a title hotly contended by a handful of competitors. It has drawn the same water for more than 200 years from the

---

GLEN KEITH

Owner:	Chivas Brothers
Age:	1983; 43%
Color:	Bright pale gold
Aroma:	Smooth and toasted with a delicate oakiness and aromatic sweetness.
Taste:	Soft, dry aromatic flavors balanced with subtle fruitiness and a warming finish.
Comment:	Dry, fresh and reviving. A nice pick-me-up.

STRATHISLA

Owner:	Chivas Brothers
Age:	12 years; 40%
Color:	Full amber
Aroma:	Complex mixture of hay and dry oakiness.
Taste:	Full and mellow with a smooth mouth-feel. A well-rounded, pleasantly nutty finish.
Comment:	Intriguing depths that require revisiting.

Fons Buliens, a spring recorded by beer-brewing Dominican monks in the twelfth century.

Chivas Brothers bought Strathisla in 1950 for a bargain £71,000 and the distillery continues to produce a zesty, forceful, botanical whisky of great character.

AULTMORE

Aultmore, which means "big burn" in Gaelic, was named to denote its ample water supply. In fact, there are so many springs and peat deposits on The Foggie Moss, the neighboring hill, that in the nineteenth century the area was awash with illicit stills.

Below: Twin kiln chimneys rising above its water wheel make Strathisla probably the most beautiful – and most photographed – of all distilleries.

Whisky from the area was always well-received in nearby towns, and Aultmore, which opened in 1897, was no exception. Despite the gathering clouds of the industry slump, production doubled within twelve months. By 1900, however, the market was overloaded with Speyside malts, but Aultmore somehow managed to limp along.

It was here, in 1952, that the first experiments were carried out to convert waste from whisky-making into high-protein cattle feed. It became one of several environmentally friendly schemes to be widely employed throughout the industry.

INCHGOWER

We're aul, and we're wracket, to work w'ed nae scruple,
Our joints they are stiff and that we do feel,
They're no like our wives tongues, for faith they're richt supple,
When they think we've been drinking the pure Tochieneal.

Malt whisky has inspired many to song, but the fortunes of Inchgower, or Tochieneal as it was originally called, became the subject of a local poem.

Tochieneal produced whisky from 1824 to 1870 until its landlords, the Earl and Countess of Seafield, who considered distilleries *infra dig*, drove it away by doubling the rent. The Wilson family, who had built a high reputation with their whisky, were forced to move their entire operation to Inchgower. There they built a model distillery with carpenter's shop, warehouse, cooperage, and "smiddy". The talk of the neighborhood, however, was a row of workers' cottages each with its own water closet, which was a minor sensation in the Highlands of the day.

The economy-conscious company raised large numbers of pig, cattle, and sheep on the by-products from the 200-acre (81ha) farm adjoining the distillery, a fitting testimony to the natural goodness of whisky.

AULTMORE

Owner:	United Distillers
Age:	12 years; 40%
Color:	Yellow gold
Aroma:	Well-composed balance of sweetness and peatiness.
Taste:	Deliciously dry with a touch of mellow fruitiness.
Comment:	Hard to find, but worth the effort.

INCHGOWER

Owner:	United Distillers
Age:	12 years; 40%
Color:	Straw-gold
Aroma:	Malty sweetness with a touch of peat.
Taste:	Medium-bodied with a mellow richness and long finish.
Comment:	A hint of salt in the finish – a reminder of the distillery's closeness to the coast.

The Malts of the River Deveron

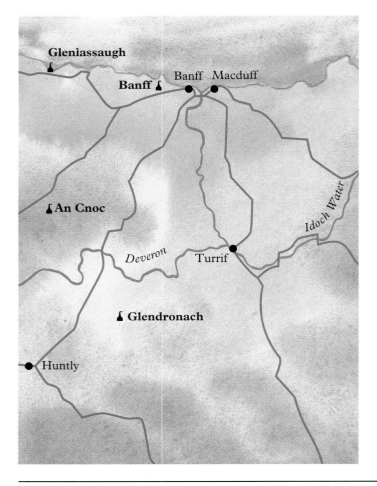

"No major cities flank its course; no aristocratic mystique clings to its banks... no clichéd verses sing its praises. Its charm is essentially elusive".

Chambers Encyclopedia of Scotland

The Deveron, or "black water", flows for eighty-two miles (132km), making it one of Scotland's longest rivers. In 1924, it yielded one of the largest salmon ever caught, weighing in at sixty-one pounds (27.6kg). However, the river's distilleries are in a class of their own.

GLENDRONACH (*glen-dron-ock*)

A rookery silhouetted high in the trees surrounding Glendronach offers visitors a rowdy reception. The colony goes back at least 200 years, when its raucous squabbling alerted illicit distillers to approaching excisemen.

The distillery, with its own working floor maltings, is one of the best examples of traditional whisky making and a pleasant air of craftsmanship pervades.

Glendronach draws its water from the Dronach Burn, but it is from maturation that the malt acquires most of its character. The earth floors of the maturation sheds and a high proportion of sherry ageing (100 per cent in one version) make their presence felt with a rich fruit and toffee sweetness.

This is an outstanding single malt of great verve and individuality with the release of occasional special editions to delight its many followers.

AN CNOC (*annock*)

This malt, bottled since 1988 under the Gaelic name of An Cnoc ("the hill"), traded for most of its life as "Knockdhu". The new name derives from the southern slopes of the hill where the distillery draws it exceptionally pure water.

Knockdhu's site was chosen in 1894 solely for its water

GLENDRONACH

Owner:	Allied Domecq
Age:	12 Years Old; 43%; matured in mix of seasoned oak and sherry wood
Color:	Rich amber
Aroma:	Malty and faintly smoky. Warm aromas of sherry and vanilla with a hint of toffee.
Taste:	Rich and complex. Lightly peated with lingering flavors of sherry, oak and smoke.

AN CNOC

Owner:	Inver House
Age:	12 Years Old; 40%
Color:	Light amber sunshine, as the distillery likes to term it.
Aroma:	Pleasantly crisp with a distinctive fragrance.
Taste:	Refined, mellow sweetness with a light, dry finish.
Comment:	A tasty all-round malt.

which had been carefully analyzed by the landowner. The supply is also piped to the local village of Knock for drinking.

An Cnoc's water possibly makes a contribution to its appealing softness, which lends the whisky an air of poise and refinement – a style which has been carefully maintained for a hundred years.

When Knockdhu opened it was considered a showpiece distillery with two steam-driven pot stills producing 2,500 gallons (11,365 litres/3000 US gallons) of spirit a week. Each staff member had a cottage with its own water closet, a development unheard of in some parts of the Highlands.

An Cnoc is a restrained, old-fashioned malt which most drinkers would find enjoyable.

BANFF AND MACDUFF

Banff lies in the ancient seaport and holiday resort at the mouth of the Deveron; MacDuff sits on the opposite shore.

MacDuff, also bottled as Glen Deveron, is a whisky in which the flavor of malt powers through. Banff, on the other hand, reflects its location with a salty whiff of sea air in the nose. Both are available largely from independent bottlers.

GLENGLASSAUGH (glen-glass-ock)

Locals who hang out their washing in the fresh sea air around Portsoy, where Glenglassaugh is made, may detect something of its distinctive aroma. The nose of this curious malt, produced on a steep slope facing the sea, has been variously described as "fresh linen" and "newly made beds", which makes it all the most mysterious why it remained out of circulation for so long. Glenglassaugh's two stills were silent for long periods, from 1907 to 1931 and for a further twenty-three years from 1936.

Although blenders have respected its contribution, Glenglassaugh has never been widely available as a single malt, despite its highly individual qualities. Given the right marketing it could still be well received.

Left: Glendronach's new 100 per cent sherry-matured malt presents a strong challenge to established Speyside whisky giants.

BANFF AND MACDUFF

Owner:	Gordon & MacPhail bottling
Age:	12 Years Old; 43%
Color:	Deep amber
Aroma:	Intense sherry with oak-vanilla.
Taste:	Rich, luscious body with a good balance of sherry and maltiness. Dry with hints of soft, peat-smokiness.

GLENGLASSAUGH

Owner:	Highland Distilleries
Age:	12 Years Old; 40%
Color:	Mid-amber
Aroma:	Delicate and slightly smoky with an unusual, fresh aroma.
Taste:	A nice smooth body with a touch of sweetness.
Comment:	For any occasion.

The Findhorn River Malts

The restless Findhorn discharges into the North Sea near the tiny fishing village of Findhorn, which was swept away in 1701 and engulfed by shifting sands on an earlier occasion.

As a whisky area, Findhorn qualifies as Speyside in its broadest definition, sharing some influences with the neighboring northern Highlands.

Its distilleries are scattered: Tomatin lies on the river's upper reaches in the Monadhliath foothills, while Benromach and Dallas Dhu are located nearer its estuary. The outsider, Royal Brackla, is made far to the west, near Nairn, combining fruitiness with coastal touches.

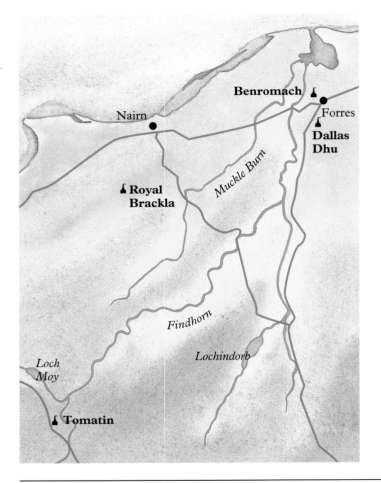

BENROMACH

This is a distilling story with a silver lining: Benromach, with its delicious body and elegant fruit and spice flavors, has been independently bottled for most of the century by merchants Gordon & MacPhail. In 1983, the distillery fell into financial problems and had to be padlocked. Ten years later, Gordon & MacPhail came to the rescue and bought it.

They plan to install new stills, restore it to its former glory and bottle Benromach under its own label for the first time since the early 1900s.

The Forres distillery, built in 1898 by architect Charles Doig, was something of an innovation: previously, distil-

BENROMACH

Owner:	Gordon & MacPhail
Age:	12 Years Old; 40%
Color:	Mid-amber
Aroma:	Delicately fresh with pleasant fruit touches.
Taste:	Rich and smoky with developing sweetness and a hint of spice.
Comment:	Satisfying aperitif.

ROYAL BRACKLA

Owner:	United Distillers
Age:	10 Years Old; 43%
Color:	Pale gold
Aroma:	Quite grassy with a nice balance of peat smoke.
Taste:	Well-rounded and fruity, turning to a dry finish.
Comment:	Pleasant for supper-time sipping.

leries had been constructed wherever possible at the foot of a hill to avoid pumping water. Modern machinery at Benromach, however, introduced methods which would enable many future distilleries to be built on the level.

It may be another ten years before the new Benromach is ready but, for enthusiasts, it will be well worth the wait.

ROYAL BRACKLA

Brackla is situated on the Cawdor Estate, the setting for Shakespeare's *Macbeth*. It earned its "Royal" epithet in 1835 when Captain William Fraser, who built the distillery in 1821, became the first distiller to be granted a royal warrant by William IV. Queen Victoria later conferred her own royal warrant in 1838.

Water for mashing and distilling has always been drawn from the Cawdor Burn. In the earliest days Brackla was not allowed to be sold within 100 miles (160km) of the distillery because of the number of illicit stills in the area. Later, in the 1860s Andrew Usher, the blending pioneer, became a partner, and Royal Brackla was used extensively in Usher's early blends. It remains in demand by modern blenders.

DALLAS DHU (*dallas-doo*)

No connection whatever with the Dallas of J.R. Ewing, but Dallas, Morayshire, where Alexander Edward of Sanquhar, an eminent Speyside laird and whisky maker, gave the distillery the Gaelic name for "black water valley".

When Dallas Dhu closed in 1983, it was earmarked by the Department of Historic Buildings for preservation as a classic small working distillery. The original barley loft, malting floor, kiln and malt mill are now visited by thousands of whisky enthusiasts each year.

Existing bottlings are from stocks of single malt set aside when the distillery closed.

Left: The River Findhorn rippling over granite scree at Tomatin, where the distillery draws its water from a burn feeding the river.

Above: The spirit store at Royal Brackla in 1890. Efficiency and cost effectiveness were highly valued by Scottish distillers.

TOMATIN (*tom-a' tin*)

The first Scottish distillery to be purchased by a Japanese company: Tahara Shuzo Co. and Okura Co., two of Tomatin's customers, bought out the company when it went into liquidation in 1986.

Tomatin is bottled as a single malt and also contributes to the company's blends. The distillery's output is an indication of its demand – it has a capacity for 2,640,000 gallons (12,000,000 litres/3,168,000 US gallons) annually from twenty-three stills – probably the highest in the industry.

The water for this sweetish, spirity single malt comes from a local burn, the Alt-Na-Frithe.

DALLAS DHU

Owner:	United Distillers
Age:	1974; 40% (Gordon & MacPhail bottling).
Color:	Amber
Aroma:	Peaty and perfumed; rather full.
Taste:	Ripe and thickly textured with dry spice in the finish.
Comment:	Limited availability.

TOMATIN

Owner:	Tahara Shuzo & Okura Co
Age:	10 Years Old; 40%
Color:	Straw
Aroma:	Dry and sharp with an aromatic smokiness.
Taste:	Soft and sweet. Well-rounded with a delicate finish.
Comment:	Substantial and worth exploring.

Malts of the Eastern Highlands

The borders of whisky regions inevitably blur. At times the line dividing Speyside from the eastern Highlands is far from distinct.

Traditionally, this region encompasses the coast and the Grampians and covers the whiskies distilled in Banffshire and adjoining parts of Aberdeenshire and Morayshire. It is an area of varying landscapes: from the hardy fishing villages that cling to the coast to the lush fields of wheat that sprawl further inland and the austere sheep farms and tumbling, salmon-rich rivers that populate the hills, two of which, the Don and Dee, reach the sea amid Aberdeen's rather po-faced granite architecture.

The whiskies vary accordingly, but while the malts of the eastern Highlands cannot rightly be said to share a cohesive style many of them here are pleasantly dry and fruity.

The region, one of the most scenic in Scotland, provides the setting for the Royal House of Balmoral, the focus of Queen Victoria's love of the Highlands and perhaps her fondness for a nightly dram. Royal Lochnagar distillery, which lies close by, lost no time securing her patronage.

The eastern Highlands were also home of Victoria's first Liberal prime minister, William Gladstone, whose father owned an estate near Old Fettercairn distillery. There is no evidence to suggest the connection gave Gladstone his affection for whisky, but he was moved nevertheless to pass legislation which greatly helped the industry through difficult times.

The distilleries of the eastern Highlands are a blend of old and new, the picturesque and the utilitarian. What they share is a collection of single malts worth exploring, one or two of which aspire to greatness.

Right: The peaceful hills and forests of the Balmoral estate. The terrain of the eastern Highlands produces deep, fruity whiskies of distinction.

A Mellow Threesome Reel

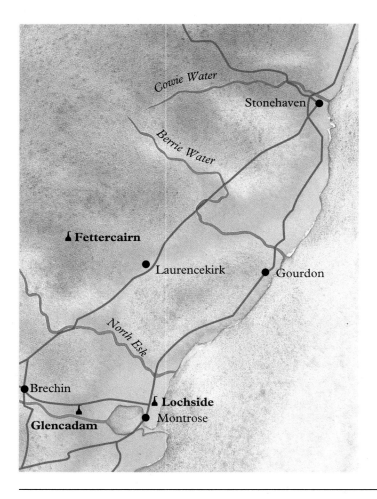

GLENCADAM

A stark little distillery on the outskirts of the sandstone town of Brechin, which rises steeply from the River Esk. Officially a city, despite its size, Brechin has long displayed a disproportionate interest in alcohol – in 1838 it boasted two breweries, two distilleries and no less than thirty-eight licensed premises.

These days Glencadam – a full, fruity whisky – is its only single malt. The two stills have the unusual feature of ascending lyne arms. These were inclined to fifteen degrees when too many "heavies" rose over from the boil, thereby affecting the whisky's character.

The local council pipes Glencadam's soft water from Loch Lee, thirty miles (48km) away, which must be the greatest distance any distillery goes for its supply. Even the cooling water, from another source, runs through thirteen miles (21km) of pipes.

Glencadam is a mellow, liqueur-quality whisky, which, though rarely bottled, is an important contributor to Stewart's Cream of the Barley.

OLD FETTERCAIRN

The British prime minister, William Ewart Gladstone, had a warm affection for the whisky industry. His father, John Gladstone, purchased the Fasque Estate at Fettercairn in the foothills of the Cairngorm mountains at the beginning of the nineteenth century when the whole area was a smuggling stronghold (though the "official" local industry was weaving). As prime minister, William Gladstone encouraged the sale of bottled malt whisky to the public and in 1853 abolished a debilitating malt tax.

Fettercairn's first owners, who had operated illicit stills deep in the mountains, built their licensed operation in 1824 when restrictions were relaxed. The distillery still draws its water from springs high in the nearby Cairngorms.

GLENCADAM

Owner:	Allied Domecq
Age:	21 Years Old; 46%
Color:	Pale amber
Aroma:	Slightly sweet with a blend of peat-smoke and fruit.
Taste:	Creamy and honeyed; a flavor of apples and summer flowers.
Comment:	Worth seeking for an unusual after-dinner malt.

Old Fettercairn, as the brand is known, is a creamy, well-rounded malt with a pleasant touch of vanilla.

Above: The unusual sandy shores and shining levels of Loch Morlich. Pure burns flow through deposits of smoky quartz to feed the Spey below.

LOCHSIDE

Although the distillery has closed and its future looks bleak, enough stocks remain to ensure that the spirit lives on for some time to come.

Lochside was built in 1957 on the site of an eighteenth-century brewery and designed for both grain and malt distillation. In 1973 it was sold to the Spanish drinks company Desilerias y Crienza del Whisky SA, which closed the continuous still operation in order to concentrate on Lochside's slightly sherried single malt.

Lochside can now only be obtained in independent bottlings. The bulk of its stock went for sale in the Spanish market and, sadly, at the time of writing the distillery seems likely to be closed permanently. Gordon & MacPhail produced a limited stock of 1966, followed by a 1981.

OLD FETTERCAIRN

Owner:	Whyte & Mackay
Age:	10 Years Old; 43%
Color:	Deep straw
Aroma:	Rich, full and almost pungent.
Taste:	Full on the palate with a silky texture and luscious malty finish.
Comment:	A delightful drink for almost any occasion.

LOCHSIDE

Owner:	MacNab Distilleries
Age:	1966; 40% (Gordon & MacPhail bottling)
Color:	Mid-amber
Aroma:	Bold and fruity with a touch of sherry.
Taste:	Mellow, well-rounded and slightly spicy with a lingering finish.
Comment:	Difficult to obtain but worth the price.

A Regal Touch

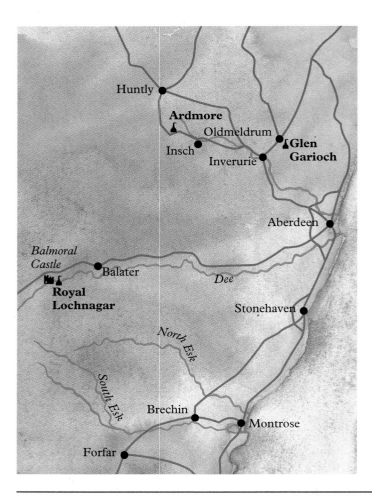

ROYAL LOCHNAGAR (*loch nay-gar*)

Plain Lochnagar, as it began, was built on the banks of the River Dee three years before Queen Victoria took up residence at Disneyesque Balmoral, which is situated half a mile round the next bend of the river.

It is said that on hearing of his new neighbors, the distillery manager lost no time in writing a note inviting the Queen and Prince Albert for a dram, adding that he only stayed open until 6pm. To his astonishment, the royal couple rolled up the next day with their children, who chased each other round the mash tuns, while their parents were offered a dram. A few days later, Victoria granted a royal warrant to Lochnagar, one of the swiftest on record. Today whisky's "Royal" appendage is no more than a link with the past – Laphroaig is the only single malt currently in possession of a royal warrant.

Royal Lochnagar's serene environment remains unspoiled, though its steam engines and paraffin lamps have long disappeared. In the summer nearby Braemar is the setting for the famous highland games, known locally as the Braemar Gathering. The distillery's water comes from springs in the foothills of Lochnagar Mountain, the inspiration for a children's story by HRH Prince Charles called "The Old Man of Lochnagar".

GLEN GARIOCH (*glen geery*)

Glen Garioch, nestling in the mellow stone village of Old Meldrum, was founded in 1797, making it one of the oldest distilleries in Scotland.

It retains its own floor maltings, generating about half its malt requirements by hand. Peat from Pitsligo Moss is burned for about four hours to produce Glen Garioch's medium-peated flavor. Surplus heat from the distilling process is harnessed to heat greenhouses where tomatoes are grown on a commercial scale.

ROYAL LOCHNAGAR

Owner:	United Distillers
Age:	12 Years Old; 40%
Color:	Pale gold
Aroma:	Lightly aromatic with traces of dried fruit.
Taste:	Quite sweet with a restrained smokiness and a discernible peppery dimension.
Comment:	Elegant and appropriately noble.

GLEN GARIOCH

Owner:	Morrison Bowmore
Age:	21 Years Old; 43%
Color:	Copper-gold
Aroma:	Smoky, with a light sherry aroma and floral, lavender notes.
Taste:	Malty and sweet with floral touches; smoky throughout with a pinch of spice.
Comment:	A warming after-dinner malt.

ARDMORE

When Teachers Highland Cream was launched in 1884 its success focused blenders' attention on the problem of securing long-term supplies of good single malts. One result was the building of Ardmore in 1898, which is still owned by the same company, now Allied Domecq, and produces 550,000 gallons (2,500,000 litres/660,000 US gallons) per annum.

Ardmore rarely makes a solo appearance as a malt, which is a pity because its buttery character is mellow and delightful. Independent bottlings, particularly an 18 Years Old for Cadenhead's, are available in limited quantities.

Above: Casks maturing at Royal Lochnagar, which had the distinction, many years ago, of producing Scotland's most expensive whisky.

Right: The annual Royal Highland Gathering has traditional clan links, but Braemar itself has become a setting over-run with souvenir shops.

The distillery closed in 1968 when its owners claimed that the spring water, used for almost 200 years, was no longer plentiful enough for their requirements. The distillery was sold and the new proprietor simply dug a well in the next field which has supplied ample water ever since.

Glen Garioch is a graceful, pleasantly smoky malt which in the past was an ingredient of Vat 69 blend.

ARDMORE

Owner:	Allied Domecq
Age:	15 Years Old; 47.5%
Color:	Deep gold
Aroma:	Malty with plenty of sweetness.
Taste:	Slight to medium peatiness; malted and honeyed with a buttery character.
Comment:	A rare bird.

The Central Highland Malts

In whisky terms, the central Highlands run from Glengoyne distillery on the southern edge of the Highlands, north to Blair Athol and Edradour near Pitlochry, and on to Dalwhinnie in the north.

Historically, the broad valley of the River Tay, with its ancient fords and cattle-crossings, formed a natural funnel for Highland and Speyside whiskies making the long journey by horse and cart and steam railway south to cities and markets in the Lowlands and over the border in England.

For this reason, perhaps, the area became particularly popular with blenders: Bells set up business in Perth, along with Dewars; while other central Highland blenders to become household names included Famous Grouse and Haig.

The region abounds with interesting whiskies and, in some cases, equally interesting distilleries. Not least among them the time capsule of Edradour, the last farm distillery with a staff of just three, where whisky is made by hand using methods of 170 years ago.

Because of Edradour's pocket-handkerchief size, one is able to view the whole whisky-making process in one room. For this reason, many fledgling drinks executives are despatched to Edradour to gain a firm grounding in how the modern industry began.

Despite its basic, almost crude techniques and miniscule output, Edradour's fragrant whisky has a wonderful depth and complexity, demonstrating what can be achieved with minimal equipment and staff. The distillery no longer has its own floor maltings (they are now a small visitors' center) but remains the gem of central Highland distilling. An opportunity to experience the craft of whisky-making in such an intimate setting should not be missed.

Right: The splendour of Loch Katrine, the inspiration for Scott's poem "The Lady of the Lake", sums up the beauty of the central Highlands.

A Tale of Two Extremes

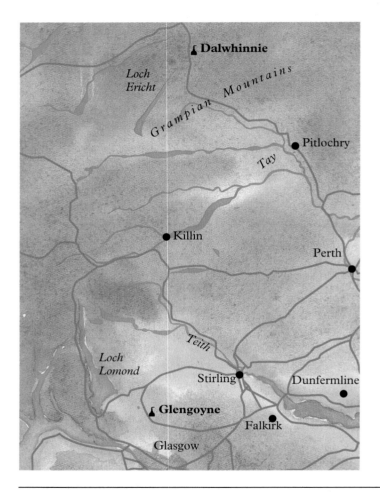

Scotland's central Highlands is a sprawling region with more than 100 miles (160km) separating remote, snowbound Dalwhinnie distillery to the north and the gentle hills of Glengoyne with almost one foot in the Lowlands. Two quite distinct whiskies from the same region – the full-flavored northerner, with layers of honey and heather, and light, unpeated Glengoyne provide a curtain-raiser to the Lowland malts to come.

DALWHINNIE

At around 1,070 feet (326m) above sea level, Dalwhinnie claims to be Scotland's highest distillery. Its location amid the winter sports scenery of the Grampians is so formidable that one writer was reminded of a fort guarding the Khyber Pass.

Weather conditions in this area are so wild and unpredictable that the distillery is designated an official Meteorological Office weather station – staff are sometimes snowbound for up to ten days during the winter, fulfilling every whisky buff's dream of being locked in a distillery.

These are the remote uplands where red deer roam and golden eagles soar. The single malt produced in this cold, crisp air is aromatic and full-bodied with a surprisingly light taste – a worthy regional choice for United Distillers' Classic Malts collection.

Dalwhinnie is steeped in history. It sits at the junction of Scotland's ancient cattle-droving roads, the same tracks once used by whisky smugglers. At nearby Ruthven barracks Bonnie Prince Charlie finally gave up his claim to the British crown and fled to Skye, his Highland army having been routed at Culloden. Out of these hard times and equally grueling climate comes a remarkably soft whisky which owes its character to dramatic seasonal changes and the fresh snow-melt used in its making. The high level of humidity at this altitude means that Dalwhinnie takes longer to mature than other regional malts.

DALWHINNIE

Owner:	United Distillers
Age:	15 Years Old; 43%
Color:	Deep amber
Aroma:	Fruity, sweet and lightly aromatic.
Taste:	Light, with what its distiller calls "an almost feminine charm" and a lingering, heather-honey finish.
Comment:	An exceptional single malt: gentle in spirit, rich in body.

The distillery was built below a fifty-foot (15m) waterfall outside the village of Killearn in 1833. In Barnard's time, barrels had to be trundled across the road to the warehouses. The buildings are still divided, but the whisky now flows in a pipe beneath the highway to the filling store.

Because of its proximity to Glasgow, Edinburgh and the tourist area of Loch Lomond, Glengoyne attracts thousands of visitors each year and even has the its own helipad.

Its whisky is light and well-rounded and about a third is matured in sherry casks. It is still manufactured by Lang Brothers who took over the distillery in 1873.

Above: Dalwhinnie distillery is situated near one of the historic roads laid by General Wade to subdue the Highlands and seek-out illicit stills.

Right: Pale, unpeated Glengoyne is a delicate malt from a distillery at the foot of a waterfall. About a third of its malt is matured in sherry casks.

GLENGOYNE

The low-lying distillery at Glengoyne – Scotland's southern-most Highland distillery – produces a pale, unpeated whisky of unusual distinction.

When Alfred Barnard visited in 1887 the distillery was known by its original spelling of "Glenguin". One of its former excisemen Arthur Tedder went on to be Chief Inspector of Excise. When his son became a peer of the realm he took the title Baron Tedder of Glenguin in memory of his father's links with Glengoyne.

GLENGOYNE

Owner:	Lang Brothers
Age:	10 Years Old; 40%
Color:	Pale gold
Aroma:	Rich malt aroma with hints of oak, apple and sherry.
Taste:	A smooth, almost creamy mouth-feel. Oak and apples with a long, clean, fruity finish.
Comment:	A good example of a beautifully balanced unpeated malt in which no particular flavor overpowers others.

Heart of the Midlands

Three distilleries nestle at the heart of the central Highlands: light-nosed Glenturret is perhaps the oldest distillery in the industry, with medium-weight Deanston, built in the 1960s, a comparative newcomer; Tullibardene, with its full aroma, has a foot in both traditions, having been extensively rebuilt in the early 1970s, yet linked to an almost forgotten eighteenth-century distillery.

DEANSTON

Deanston's is situated at Doune, seven miles (11km) from Stirling, which makes it one of the most southerly of the Highland distilleries.

A cotton mill, designed by spinning pioneer Richard Arkwright, was built on the site in 1785. It wasn't until 1965 that the the former weaving shed was turned into a maturation warehouse and the old mill was converted into a distillery.

The whisky was originally bottled as Deanston Mill and described by its owners as "a spirit of hidden vigor and an elegant palate". Since then, the malt has had its name shortened, but its soft, delicate style thankfully remains unchanged.

Deanston closed during the industry's troubled years of the mid-1980s, but reopened and was sold to its current owners Burn Stewart in 1990.

The distillery draws its water from the River Teith which retains as much functional importance as it had in the 1700s when it powered the cotton mill. Today the river drives hydro-electric turbines to generate Deanston's power supply.

GLENTURRET

One of a handful of Highland pocket-handkerchief sized distilleries claiming to be among the smallest allowed by law (also see Edradour and Speyside-Drumguish).

Glenturret's real distinction lies not in its diminutive size, but in the evidence that it may well be the oldest distillery in

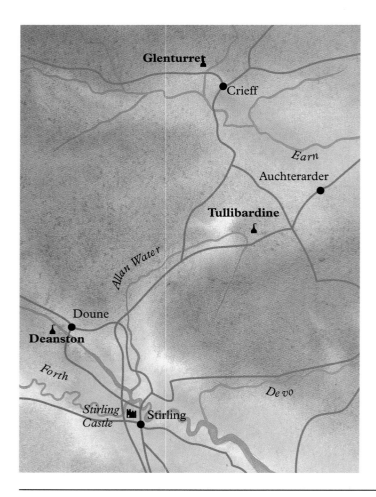

DEANSTON

Owner:	Burn Stewart
Age:	12 Years Old; 40%
Color:	Pale amber
Aroma:	Fragrant and fruity with a touch of dryness.
Taste:	Smooth and malty with a sweet, lingering aftertaste.
Comment:	A refreshing pre-dinner pick-me-up.

the Scotch whisky industry (Littlemill is the closest contender). There has been a distillery on the site since 1775 and illicit stills as far back as 1717.

After a checkered past in which Glenturret was completely dismantled in 1929 and turned over to storing farm stock, its fortunes revived in the 1950s.

It remains a hand-made whisky with a tiny production staff which has seldom exceeded two. The distillery's most celebrated employee was Towser the cat who entered the *Guinness Book of Records* for catching 28,899 mice. Towser died aged twenty-four in 1987 with a fearsome reputation that extended to hunting rabbits and pheasants, in addition to distillery-patrolling duties.

Glenturret's smooth, rounded, medium-sweet malt is bottled at 8, 10, 12, 15, 21 and 25 Years Old, with several vintages.

TULLIBARDINE

A favorite at the nineteenth hole – Tullibardine takes its name from the famous moor on which Gleneagles golf course was constructed. The distillery was designed in 1949 by William Delmé Evans whose austere, functional but attractive lines may also be found at Jura and Glenallachie distilleries.

Despite the fact that it was constructed in the mid-twentieth century, Tullibardine's water supply from the Danny Burn has an impressive pedigree. The distillery was built in the grounds of a seventeenth-century brewery, and Highland Spring bottled water also hails from Blackford village.

Tullibardine is produced from two pairs of stills and the earliest records of its water go back to 1488, when an earlier Tullibardine brewery was commissioned to provide ale for one of Scotland's grandest occasions, the coronation of King James IV at Scone.

Many Highland malts have a delicate aroma but Tullibardine's is more subtle than most. Its flavor, too, has quite profound depths of fruit and spices.

Left: The late Towser, Glenturret's record-breaking cat. Bowmore, on Islay, also has a famous cat which sleeps in the extinguished peat oven.

Below: Glenturret's pale, creamy 12 Years Old is the most popular malt from the Crieff distillery. Older versions up to 25 years are available.

GLENTURRET

Owner:	Glenturret
Age:	12 Years Old; 40%
Color:	Light gold
Aroma:	Medium-bodied and malty sweet with a slight hint of sherry.
Taste:	Like velvet on the palate; creamy rich with a long, stimulating finish.
Comment:	A beautiful malt worth deeper investigation.

TULLIBARDINE

Owner:	Whyte & Mackay
Age:	10 Years Old; 40%
Color:	Grapey gold
Aroma:	Honey-melon with a hint of Bourbon. Unexpectedly intense.
Taste:	Rich, spicy and full-flavored. Creamy textured with an elegant finish.
Comment:	An intriguing malt with an almost winey feel. For stimulating the appetite.

To Blend or Not To Blend...

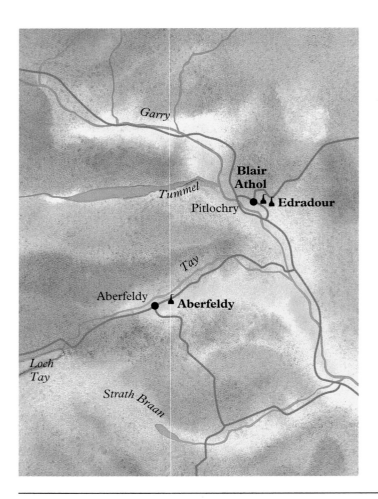

The central Highlands is blending country and, appropriately, two of the region's home-grown malts lie at the heart of famous blends. Blair Athol is a well-known contributor to Bells Extra Special and Aberfeldy an important component of Dewar's White label. At the other extreme lies The Edradour, with an output so small that it can barely spare any for blending at all.

ABERFELDY

This whisky, which almost sounds Welsh, was created in 1896 by the Dewars of Perth, one of the industry's most colorful families. A century on, it still supplies Dewar's White Label, one of the biggest-selling blends in the United States.

The Dewars took a feu of 12 acres (5ha) from the Marquis of Breadalbane to build the distillery, only a couple of miles from the farm where John Dewar was born.

One crucial advantage of the site was the excellent water supply from Pitilie Burn, which had served Pitilie Distillery until it closed in 1867. Today, Aberfeldy's water is still drawn from the ruins of Pitilie's old distillery to ensure continuity and quality.

John Dewar's son Tommy had a tremendous impact on the company, expanding it worldwide with the appointment of thirty-two agents in twenty-six countries. At home, he built a new headquarters in Perth alongside the North British Railway's goods station. From here, he ran a branchline directly to his beloved Aberfeldy, providing a door-to-door service for his rich, full single malt.

BLAIR ATHOL

Back in 1689, when William III's English army was defeated by the Scots, victory was ascribed in no small part to "the mellow barley bree from the cavern of Ben Vrackie that warmed the hearts and strengthened the arms of the Highlanders at

ABERFELDY

Owner:	United Distillers
Age:	15 Years Old; 43%
Color:	Pale amber
Aroma:	Medium-peated with a pleasant touch of vanilla.
Taste:	Full, firm and well-rounded. A smooth, soothing finish.
Comment:	Difficult to find.

*Above: The Edradour, outside
Pitlochry, is the last of the small
farm-style distilleries and
tremendously popular with visitors.*

Ben Vrackie. Aldour – after the burn – was the name given to the original distillery on the site in 1798.

Blair Athol is a distinctive dram with an abundance of flavor, which has managed to sell consistently in both England and Scotland for many years.

THE EDRADOUR

Blair Athol is a near neighbor of this tiny distillery where time has almost stood still. The Edradour's huddle of whitewashed buildings with their bright red doors look like a painted backdrop from Brigadoon.

The Edradour is the last of the old farm distilleries, where steaming draff is shovelled by hand onto the local farmer's tractor-drawn cart. Output is minute – little more than 600 gallons (2,700 litres/720 US gallons) a week. Any smaller, says the manager, and the stills would have to be hidden away in the hillside.

Around 2,000 cases of this honey-sweet, gloriously flavored single malt go for sale each year, the rest is top dressing for House of Lords, a light, fragrant blend sold at the bar of the House of Lords, and occasionally duty free.

Both the distillery and the whisky are proof that "small is beautiful" – an idyllic setting at the foot of a hill with a clear burn bubbling between the buildings; a smooth malt with touches of butter and fruit.

Killiecrankie." The "barley bree" in question was uisge beatha from the Vale of Atholl. The distillery stands at the gateway to the Highlands and its whisky straddles two styles, combining a light body with a pleasant touch of peat.

Blair Athol distillery dates back to 1825 and is one of Pitlochry's busiest tourist attractions, bringing in 100,000 visitors a year. It takes its water from the Allt Dour Burn (The Burn of the Otter) flowing from a spring 2760ft (841m) up on

---

BLAIR ATHOL

Owner:	United Distillers
Age:	8 Years Old; 40%
Color:	Bright gold
Aroma:	Light, clean and well composed. Quite aromatic.
Taste:	Sweet, giving way to layers of spice and an elegant finish.
Comment:	Nice before a meal.

THE EDRADOUR

Owner:	Campbell Distillers (Pernod Ricard)
Age:	10 Years Old; 40%
Color:	Deep gold
Aroma:	Like stepping into a Dickensian sweet shop – honey, sugared almonds, whiffs of peppermint twists and gingerbread.
Taste:	Wonderfully smooth and creamy mouthfeel with a buttery flavor and a touch of fruit.
Comment:	A gem – and not too difficult to track down.

The West Highlands & Western Isles

*"A man of the Hebrides... as soon as he appears in the morning,
swallows a glass of whisky; yet they are not a drunken race,
at least I was never present at much intemperance."*

Dr. Johnson, *A Journey to the Hebrides*

Whisky's western Highlands run north from Glasgow the entire length of Scotland, with the exception of Islay and the Campbeltown Peninsula whose styles are distinctive enough to be considered regions in their own right (see pages 100-109).

Considering its size, the mainland area contains surprisingly few distilleries. The Hebridean whiskies on Jura, Skye and Mull combine robust coastal qualities with an attractive intensity, while those on the mainland are quieter and a little more discreet.

Among the most interesting is Oban, which is a curious town dominated by McCaig's Folly, an unfinished replica of the Colosseum conjured up by a Victorian banker to provide work for unemployed local craftsmen.

Directly below the ruin lies a distillery producing an equally curious malt. Neither Highland, nor Island, but an harmonious balance of the two. The Highland presence exerts itself in soft water from three mountain lochs and a gentle suggestion of peat; while from the Islands come marine influences brought by the salt air which pervades its warehouse.

What the region lacks in distillery numbers, it makes up for with a fascinating range of malts, from rugged, weatherbeaten Island offerings to softer, more subtle Highland styles.

*Right: Jura's lightly peated whisky
has the kind of highly individual
character that is found in malts of
the West Highlands and Islands.*

Malts of the Western Isles

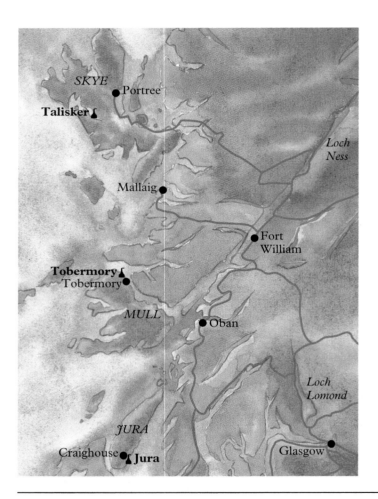

The beautiful whiskies of the Western Isles may not have a collective style, but their very individuality deserves a classification of its own.

JURA

The sun rising over the spectacular Paps of Jura is a dramatic sight. Behind the Mountain of the Sound, the Mountain of Gold and the Sacred Mountain, where green moorland runs down to a half-moon bay, stands Jura Distillery.

It was established in 1810, but records of a distillery on the island go back to the end of the seventeenth century, and an illicit still was reputed to have been there as early as 1502.

This is one of Scotland's most mysterious and least known islands. A place of tranquillity where red deer outnumber the 180-strong population by twenty to one. The novelist George Orwell wrote *1984* here.

Jura is a light, but extremely characterful whisky, shaped by its stills, which are designed to prevent heavier compounds passing over into the new spirit. According to the people who market the whisky, it is "as memorable as the island itself". A romanticized view but, for once, difficult to argue with.

TOBERMORY

Tobermory Distillery squats at the water's edge where the wooded hills of Mull tumble steeply to the sea. The whisky is dry and peaty and uses only Scottish barley.

Tobermory is a vatted malt, mainly due to an oft-interrupted history of ownership which has not permitted seamless distilling and maturation.

The distillery was closed from 1930 to 1972, and then hesitantly opened for three years, before being bought out yet again. Wisely, the new owners have made the best of the distillery's produce by bottling a vatted malt which marries older Tobermory with younger whisky from elsewhere.

JURA

Owner:	Whyte & Mackay
Age:	10 Years Old; 40%
Color:	Pale amber
Aroma:	Rich and full; quite complex with almond notes.
Taste:	Distinguished, with a pleasantly fruity oiliness and a hint of smoke.
Comment:	An intriguing malt with lingering flavors.

Mull's distillery was originally called Ledaig, a name it retained until 1978. Single malts under this label are available from independents (Cadenhead's offer a 23 Years Old) and as limited quantity vintages from the distillery.

ARRAN

This is the newest and, at the time of writing, as yet unavailable Island whisky. The island of Arran, which is tucked between the Mull of Kintyre and the mainland, was renowned for its malt whisky until the nineteenth century.

The new Arran single malt, due for release in 2001, is the dream of former managing director of Chivas Brothers, Harold Currie, who opened the island's first legal distillery for 150 years at Lochranza.

TALISKER

The Isle of Skye is one of the most scenic of the Western Isles. Talisker, its only distillery, sits by the sea in an idyllic setting.

It was founded in 1830 by the MacAskill brothers who adopted one of the nastier vices of the Scottish landowning classes. Wooed by the prospect of high profits, they evicted

crofting families and turned the land over to sheep farming. Talisker, named after Hugh MacAskill's house, developed a more worthy reputation. Its merits prompted the poet R.L. Stevenson to pen this rhyme in 1830.

"The king o'drinks; as I conceive it,
Talisker, Isla or Glenlivet."
From "The Scotsman's Return from Abroad"

The distillery has changed hands many times, but its intense, peppery whisky remains one of the most distinctive in Scotland and continues to prosper. Talisker is an acquired taste – ideal as a winter-warmer on a cold day – and one whisky buffs are taking to in increasing numbers.

Left: Skye's peat beds supply local crofts for fuel and its only distillery, Talisker, which produces an equally warming whisky.

Below: Talisker's main expression is the 10 Years Old, which leaves no doubt as to its island origins; vintages are available from independents.

TOBERMORY

Owner:	Burn Stewart
Age:	No statement; 40% (vatted)
Color:	Light amber
Aroma:	Fresh, dry and lightly peated with smoky nose.
Taste:	Smooth, fruity and well-rounded, but without the Island intensity of its more assertive stable mate, Ledaig Single Malt.
Comment:	Ledaig, which is rich and spicy with a floral nose and a peppery finish, beats it for character and unbridled flavor.

TALISKER

Owner:	United Distillers
Age:	10 Years Old; 45.8%
Color:	Pale gold
Aroma:	Pungent, peaty and powerful with a slight sweetness.
Taste:	Seaweed, pepper, sweet-and-sour flavors building to a warming finish.
Comment:	The taste has been accurately described as exploding in the mouth. Wonderful after a winter walk.

Gateways to the Isles

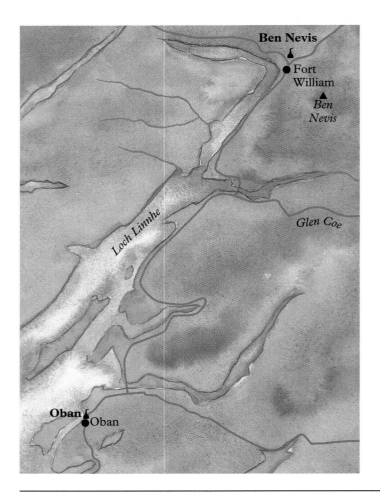

"In the thin glory of the mountain air the spirit awakens and thrills to influences beyond perception, influences which were at the beginning and will be at the end of history."

Hugh Quigley on the Western Highlands
The Highlands of Scotland, 1936

Oban and Fort William lie where the wild, cold Highlands meet the warm Gulf Stream on Scotland's western seaboard. Two ports guard the gateways to the Isles with equally commanding whiskies.

OBAN

The port of Oban grew up around its distillery, which sits near the waterfront, facing Mull and the ferry routes to the Western Isles. The community was little more than a hamlet when the distillery was established in 1794 by Hugh Stevenson, who developed most of the locality with his brother, quarrying slate and building houses and boats. The town grew up around it, resulting in the unusual sight of a distillery in the high street.

This distinctive "malt and salt" whisky has a 200-year tradition of quality which the distillery manager is not anxious to change. He had a traumatic time in 1997 when part of the old spirit still had to be replaced, the neck having become paper-thin with constant use. To ensure there was no change in flavor, the new section was made identical to the old.

Oban single malt used to be matured for twelve years, but is now left in oak for fourteen, the extra time thought to improve its rather complex character. It carries a delicate whiff of peat and a long smooth finish, positioning it somewhere between a Speyside and an Islay.

The whisky is a curious mixture of styles, which the distillery's manager Ian Williams puts down to its location: "We're right at the edge of the Highlands and a short sail from the Islands," he says. "Oban has the characteristics of both.

OBAN

Owner:	United Distillers
Age:	14 Years Old; 43%
Color:	Yellow gold
Aroma:	Delicately peaty, rich and complex.
Taste:	Medium-sweet with a creamy texture and long smooth finish.
Comment:	A unique combination of Highland and Island influences. Ideal for any occasion.

Look at a map of Scotland and we're bang in the middle of the whisky-making regions."

BEN NEVIS

Fort William was originally home to two distilleries, only one of which is now in production. Glenlochy closed in 1983 and its light peaty malt is available these days only from specialist bottlers. Ben Nevis, however, is much in demand, particularly in the Far East, thanks to the efforts of its Japanese owners, Nikka.

Fort William, originally an English outpost in the struggle to subdue rebellious Jacobites, is overshadowed by Ben Nevis, which, at just over 4000 feet (1,219m), is Britain's highest mountain. The distillery takes its water from the Allt a'Mhuilinn ("mill burn"), which is renowned for its snow-cold and exceptionally pure water.

Ben Nevis produces a rich and rather herbal 19 Years Old malt, which is quite magnificent and eclipsed only by a liqueur-smooth 26 Years Old of exquisite character.

The distillery was founded by "Long John" Macdonald, who stood at six feet four inches (1.93m) tall and later gave his name to the whisky blend. In 1864 a travel writer said of him, "This gentleman, the distiller of the place, was the tallest man I ever beheld... and must in his youth have been of incomparable physique".

However, the distillery's most colorful owner was undoubtedly Joseph Hobbs. Hobbs, who took over the distillery in 1955, was a swashbuckling Scot who had put down roots in Canada and made (and lost) a fortune bootlegging across the border during Prohibition. Ben Nevis was one of his many of Scottish distillery acquisitions. His former home, Inverlochy Castle, is now a luxury hotel.

Left: Oban is a highly individual single malt with its face to the islands, but its feet firmly rooted in the Highlands.

Below: Sunrise on the slopes below Ben Nevis. The single malt produced here has all the rich aromas of a fruit cake mixture.

BEN NEVIS

Owner:	Nikka
Age:	19 Years Old; 46%.
Color:	Deep amber.
Aroma:	Full and rich with notes of dried fruit.
Taste:	Flavor in abundance. Very smooth and characterful; sweet with a lingering finish.
Comment:	Worth seeking out.

The Northern Highland Malts

The distilleries of the northern Highlands, that gaunt finger of windswept land pointing towards Orkney, all lie on the coast, or close to it. This is the most sparsely inhabited region of western Europe – the last great wilderness, it has been called. Grey seas make their presence felt; wrecks litter Scapa Flow in the Orkneys; eider duck bob unperturbed in the vast swell round the oil terminals of Cromarty and Moray; dolphins, porpoises and seals draw thousands of sightseers each year.

Yet the handful of distilleries clinging to the coast are influenced less by the sea than by the peat and heather of the mountains behind them. For these are not the nautical malts of the West with their ozone intensity. Northern Highland malt whiskies are often pleasantly spicy with subtle flowery aromas. Only occasionally do they carry a salt tang to give away their coastal location.

Perhaps the most famous northern malt is Glenmorangie, which, it never tires of telling us, has the tallest stills in the Highlands at sixteen feet and ten and a quarter inches (4.9m). The result is a light, fragrant, delightfully aromatic whisky thoroughly deserving of its acclaim.

Glenmorangie's experiments with maturation in its Wood Finish Range have attracted recent attention. The whiskies are matured in oak for at least twelve years before being racked into casks previously used for port, madeira or sherry to finish them.

Less voluptuous, but no less interesting, are the big, honest whiskies of the Orkneys, Scotland's northernmost distilling area. Highland Park and Scapa proudly shout their island identity.

The northern Highlands is a region of outstanding malts, some of celebrity status, others more retiring but with equally fascinating characters to offer nevertheless.

Right: The low, treeless landscape of Orkney, with Hoy in the distance. The island group has two distilleries – Highland Park and Scapa.

Orkney, the Isles Where Time Began

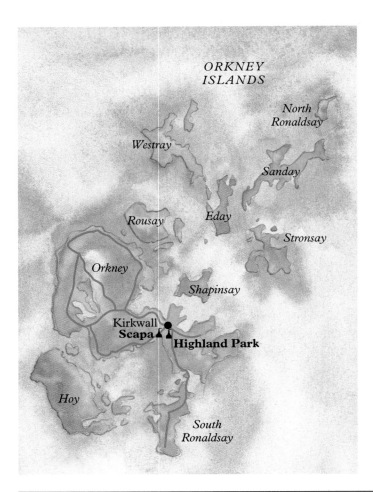

ORKNEY ISLANDS

North Ronaldsay

Westray

Sanday

Rousay   *Eday*

Stronsay

Orkney

Shapinsay

Kirkwall
Scapa   **Highland Park**

Hoy

South Ronaldsay

Orkney's archeological treasures, in the form of buried Neolithic villages and standing stones, are ranked alongside Stonehenge and the Pyramids of Egypt. The sixty-seven islands have been continuously occupied by man for 5,000 years, and for the past 3,000 years the landscape has been indelibly shaped by farming.

In the long march of history, Orcadian whisky has been distilled for a mere handful of centuries. The islands only became part of Scotland in the fifteenth century and their two distilleries retain uniquely different styles. Highland Park has by far the biggest overseas sales, but Scapa is more popular on the islands themselves.

HIGHLAND PARK

The distillery lies only a few miles from its neighbor, Scapa, yet the two differ considerably. However, what they have in common is a long tradition of whisky making. Smuggling and illicit stills flourished on the islands which were difficult to police and populated by Orcadians who held the unanimous view that high taxes imposed from the mainland should be ignored wherever possible.

One illicit distiller from Kirkwall, Magnus Eunson, hid his casks beneath the church pulpit with no apparent objection from the minister. Highland Park stands on the same spot where his whisky was made.

The distillery was established in 1823 and draws its water from clear springs nearby. It still operates its own malting floor, for which it extracts a distinctive shallow-cut, rooty peat from its own moss nearby.

Highland Park is a medium-peated, silky smooth malt, which seems ideally suited to virtually any occasion. Sales have climbed steadily in recent years, mainly because of its versatile, well-balanced character, which particularly appeals to newcomers to malt whisky.

HIGHLAND PARK

Owner:	Highland Distilleries
Age:	8 Years Old; 40% (Gordon & MacPhail bottling)
Color:	Glowing amber
Aroma:	Delicate, with beautifully balanced smoke and heather sweetness.
Taste:	Equally good flavor balance. Full malt delivery; rounded smoky sweetness and a nice honey-smooth finish.
Comment:	A medium, velvety malt that goes down well anytime.

The distillery is justly proud of its water from nearby Lingro Burn – staff used to bottle the water to take home before the distillery scaled down production, and the manager still insists it makes the perfect cup of tea.

Scapa, like its neighbor, is very much an island distillery, with barley brought in by boat along with fuel to fire the stills. It is now being actively marketed as a single malt by the distillery and more should be heard of its smooth, gently smoky qualities which carry a pleasant pinch of sea salt.

Above: Highland Park maturation warehouse, where casks mature in the cool air of the world's most northerly distillery.

Right: Scapa, considered by some to be the real Orcadian malt. Highland Park exceeds it in terms of worldwide sales, but Scapa is the locals' choice.

SCAPA

The rather bleak, wind-blasted distillery overlooks the cold waters of Scapa Flow, where German warships were scuttled at the end of the World War I. In the World War II the distillery was swept by fire and would have been destroyed but for the the efforts of sailors who fought the flames.

SCAPA	
Owner:	Allied Domecq
Age:	10 Years Old; 43%
Color:	Rich amber
Aroma:	Deceptively deep, underpinned with a pleasant peatiness.
Taste:	Silky and well-rounded; faintly floral with a slight hint of salt.
Comment:	Very acceptable, despite being traditionally eclipsed by its neighbor.

Malts of the Northeast Coast

"Glenmorangie, the Bible and Shakespeare."
Traveller Eric Newby's survival kit
Desert Island Discs, BBC Radio, 1982

OLD PULTENEY (*pult-nay*)

The most northerly distillery on mainland Britain, just twenty miles (32km) from John O'Groats. The distillery lies in Wick, the town Robert Louis Stevenson said "lives for herring"; its urban location reminiscent of Oban Distillery, which is also, unusually, on the high street.

Old Pulteney attributes its flavor in part to its two stills. It is reported to be one of the fastest-maturing of all malt whiskies and is bottled accordingly at a slightly younger age (8 Years Old; 40%).

Old Pulteney has been famously described as the "Manzanilla of the North", a reference to its smack of salt, which is similar in style to the sherries matured in coastal warehouses near Jerez.

Pulteney was founded in 1826 at a time when 10,000 people were employed in the Wick herring industry. When fishing declined, many coopers who made herring barrels were employed by the distillery.

CLYNELISH (*klyn-leash*)

Clynelish is a modern 1960s-style distillery (it reminded the late whisky writer Gordon Brown of a biscuit factory), but its roots reach back to 1819.

It produces a curious, idiosyncratic malt which, at first taste, appears to come from the other side of Scotland. It shares many of the big, powerful characteristics associated with the Western Isles. But such are the delightful quirks of whisky making. In contrast, Clynelish's nearest neighbors on the coast, Balblair and Glenmorangie, display hardly any seashore characteristics at all.

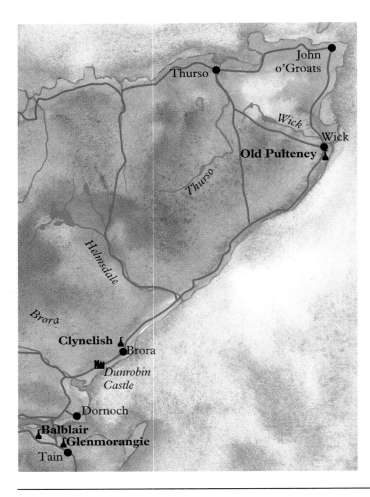

OLD PULTENEY

Owner:	Inver House
Age:	8 Years Old; 40%
Color:	Yellow amber
Aroma:	Pleasingly pungent with a whiff of ozone.
Taste:	Clean on the palate with an appealing smokiness. A tang of salt turning into a warming finish.
Comment:	A pre-dinner pick-me-up.

CLYNELISH

Owner:	United Distillers
Age:	12 Years Old; 40%
Color:	Rich gold
Aroma:	Slightly fruity with a strong touch of the seashore.
Taste:	A little smoky with a nice balance of sweetness and dryness.
Comment:	Slightly easier to obtain since the owners marketed it as a heritage malt.

GLENMORANGIE (*glen m'ranjie*)

The giant of the northern Highlands, in sales, marketing and its enormously tall stills. Despite its stature, Glenmorangie is one of the smallest operating Highland distilleries, employing (lest anyone is still unaware) the "sixteen men of Tain".

Methods have changed little and it pursues perhaps the most rigorous "wood regime" in the industry. Oaks are selected from the Ozarks while still growing, felled at 100 years old and seasoned for eighteen months before being filled with bourbon to condition them.

Glenmorangie's hard water from Tarlogie Springs bubbles through limestone layers to prove that the hardest water makes the softest whisky. Glenmorangie is noted for its delicate, fruity, almost smoky aroma and creamy taste. It is considered one of a handful of malts delicious taken neat.

BALBLAIR

Balblair lies a short distance from Glenmorangie and very much in its shadow. It is a light, "compact" whisky, nicely composed with few flavors scrambling to dominate.

This balance has earned respect among its neighbors. Millionaire Andrew Carnegie stocked Balblair in his cellars at nearby Skibo Castle (now Peter de Savary's rural retreat for the rich and famous). The distillery's other neighbors, the Al Fayed brothers, are understood to have celebrated their purchase of Harrods with Balblair for their guests.

For many years it was used mainly for blending and rarely bottled outside independents. Now, under the ownership of Inver House, it looks set for revival with new plans for bottling and major release as a single.

The original distillery cost £750 and was built by the Marquess of Stafford, later to become the Duke of Sutherland, to revitalize tenant farms, which eked a living supplying illicit distillers. Sadly, sound management succumbed to greed and the marquess evicted 15,000 tenants, burning many of their crofts behind them, to lease his 500,000 acres (202,350ha) of land to sheep farmers.

The old Clynelish distillery was replaced in 1967, retaining the same water supply from Clynemilton Burn. For a brief period in the 1970s it traded as Brora Distillery.

GLENMORANGIE

Owner:	MacDonald & Muir.
Age:	10 Years Old; 40%.
Color:	Pale gold.
Aroma:	Delicate, sophisticated and clean with complex floral notes and a light smokiness.
Taste:	Fresh and creamy; exquisitely balanced with notes of fruit, honey, flowers, nuts and spices.
Comment:	The Tain giant; never fails to please.

BALBLAIR

Owner:	Inver House.
Age:	10 Years Old; 57% (Gordon & MacPhail bottling).
Color:	Rich amber.
Aroma:	Delicate, smoky sweetness.
Taste:	Clean, fresh and creamy; spicy dryness and a long finish.
Comment:	New owners assessing stock in 1997 to determine the premium age for Balblair to be relaunched.

Distilleries & Dolphins

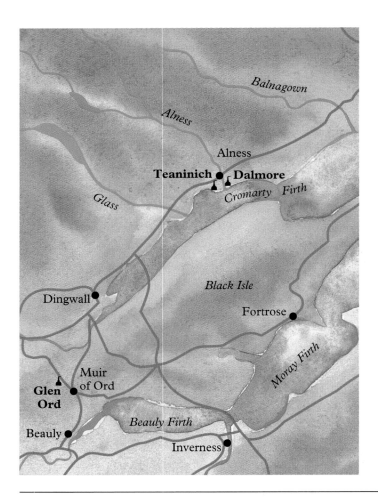

The Cromarty Firth is a blend of wild nature, agriculture and industry. Hundreds of sightseers gather at the narrows of the Firth to watch bottle-neck dolphins and harbor porpoises play. Further out, Risso's dolphins and whales are occasionally seen within a few miles of oil installation repair depots and the long, low outline of the barley-rich Black Isle.

The area has three single malt distilleries. One of them, Glen Ord, is the only survivor of nine distilling sites (mostly illegal) on the Black Isle.

DALMORE

White & Mackay have been distilling at Dalmore since 1960, but the distillery has produced whisky since 1839. Most of it goes for blending, but it is increasingly being bottled as a single malt. This is a full-bodied, intense whisky with a nice bite which goes down well locally in the wild weather of the Cromarty Firth.

Distilling began on a farm owned by Hong Kong entrepreneur and adventurer Alexander Jardine of the trading company Jardine Matheson. Under the stewardship of the Mackenzie brothers, Dalmore became the first Scottish malt whisky to be exported to Australia, and it has since continued to prosper. The stag's head of the Mackenzie clan still features on the Dalmore label.

The site for the distillery was chosen in one of Scotland's richest barley-producing regions; its water comes from the River Alness, otherwise known as "the river of tears", which flows from the Loch of Gildermory.

Dry, smoky and spicy with a nice touch of sherry sweetness, this is a classic north Highland malt.

TEANINICH (*tee-an-inich*)

One of Teaninich's claims to fame is as a contributor to Drambuie liqueur. This is a malt loved by blenders for its soft

DALMORE

Owner:	White & Mackay
Age:	12 Years Old; 40%
Color:	Golden mahogany
Aroma:	Profound with a malty elegance and a hint of Oloroso.
Taste:	Muscular with a citric mouth-feel; wonderfully sherry-smooth throughout.
Comment:	A big malt with a pleasingly long finish.

THE DALMORE
SINGLE
HIGHLAND MALT
SCOTCH WHISKY
AGED 12 YEARS
70cl   THE DALMORE DISTILLERY SCOTLAND
DISTILLED, AGED & BOTTLED
IN SCOTLAND   40%vol

Right: Teaninich's squat, bulbous stills produce well-rounded malt whisky for Drambuie liqueur. It is occasionally bottled as a self.

texture and clean finish. A high volume from its twelve stills go for blending.

Since it was extensively rebuilt in the 1970s, there is nothing to be seen of the original 1817 distillery. But, of course, a distillery does not have to be old to make fine whisky. Teaninich, a sprawling operation covering twenty acres (9ha) is blessed with a good supply of process and cooling water from Dairywell Spring.

Barnard described it in 1887 as "beautifully situated on the margin of the sea" as it sits compactly on the shores of the Cromarty Firth. The porpoises which play in the waters feature on its label.

Teaninich is rather elusive as a bottled single malt, but worth the trouble to look out for. It possesses a strong character, which makes its presence felt from nose to finish.

GLEN ORD

Glen Ord has traded under several names in the past: Ord, The Ord, and Glenordie, to mention a few. Thankfully, it now appears to have discovered its own identity and seems destined for great things.

Its owners, United Distillers, certainly think so and have injected £750,000 into marketing it as a self. Only 5 per cent of Glen Ord is bottled, the rest goes into Dewar's blends. For around 150 years, it was mainly consumed locally. Muir of Ord residents would trek miles "up the glen for a jug of Ord". Despite its parochial past, it has the unmistakable aura of a star in the making.

The distillery, tucked in a fold of hills on the Earl of Cromarty's estate, has become one of the biggest tourist attractions in the northern Highlands. More than 30,000 visitors a year travel to view its six majestic stills gushing 13,200 gallons (60,000 litres/15,840 US gallons) of spirit a week.

Glen Ord's broad appeal lies in its light peating, long maturation, smoothness and delicate influence of sherry oak.

The distillery has the highest proportion of women in key production positions of any in Scotland, following the tradition of women distillers at Laphroaig and Littlemill.

TEANINICH

Owner:	United Distillers
Age:	10 Years Old; 43%
Color:	Pale gold
Aroma:	Gently smoky with layers of spice and apple.
Taste:	Soft and well-rounded with an abundance of subtle flavors and a warming finish.
Comment:	Worth contemplating at leisure.

GLEN ORD

Owner:	United Distillers
Age:	12 Years Old; 40%
Color:	Rich amber
Aroma:	Lightly peated with a beautiful balance
Taste:	Very smooth indeed with an even distribution of flavor. Clean on the palate with a nice touch of north Highland spice.
Comment:	Style alone should elevate it to the supermarket Top Ten.

The Islay Malts

Islay (*eye-la*) is a place of great distinction. Twenty-five miles (40km) long, it is the most southerly of the Western Isles and exposed to Atlantic weather – travel west from Islay and the next port of call is Newfoundland. Historically, it was the administrative center for the Lords of the Isles.

The rock formations of which the island is composed are the oldest in Scotland and, indeed, among the most ancient on the planet. Islay's tranquil landscape is covered by a thick mantle of peat thousands of years old, which, unlike the forest-based peat beds of Speyside, is suffused with seaweed and wind-driven brine.

The island is extremely fertile; it once produced its own barley in quantity despite high on-shore winds. Home-grown grain, together with its peat and distinctive water, made Islay a whisky-making heaven. In fact, in the whisky canon, Islay is almost as important as Speyside.

Distilling in Scotland may even have been started in the region by monks from Ireland, less than seventeen miles (27km) away. In the eighteenth and nineteenth centuries the island's illicit spirits were in great demand on the mainland. Today, Islay's eight distilleries produce malts of great character with varying degrees of peatiness.

This is a place of hardy, independent people; rugged coastlines; long strands; rich harvests from the sea and land; and awash with wonderful single malts, among them the most outstanding in the Scotch whisky spectrum.

Right: Port Ellen, gateway to the southern shores of Islay, where some of the world's smokiest, most flavorsome whiskies are produced.

Southern Islay Malts

The whiskies of the island's rocky, storm-lashed southern tip are synonymous with iodine, ozone and salt air. Oily, pungent, smoky and assertive – not malts for beginners, but wonderful to meet all the same.

LAPHROAIG (la-froyg)

Laphroaig is marketed as the world's most challenging single malt. Love it or hate it, the advertisements say, there are no half measures.

Laphroaig, in Gaelic "the beautiful hollow by the broad bay", lies directly on the beach and faces an annual storm damage bill of £30,000. In bad weather the seaweed is airborne, hanging from roof gutters and often piled high against the still room door. Small wonder, then, that this beachcomber malt has a distinct tang of the sea.

Laphroaig, which was established in 1815 and waited another ten years before taking out a licence, retains its own floor maltings, patrolled by a resident family of stoats to keep field mice at bay. It is heavily peated and, despite being an acquired taste, is one of the best-selling malts.

The distillery had the distinction of having had the most celebrated woman manager in the industry, Bessie Williamson. Without her high standards of quality and continuity, Laphroaig might not have been the success it is today.

LAGAVULIN (laga-voolin)

Situated a mile away from Laphroaig on the shore facing the headland castle of Dunnyveg, one of the harbor strongholds of the Lords of the Isles. In the eighteenth and nineteenth centuries this was an area teeming with illicit stills and notoriously difficult for excisemen to police. At one time Lagavulin was a collection of nine or ten smugglers' bothies around the small bay set behind the castle.

The distillery was founded in 1816 and had the distinction

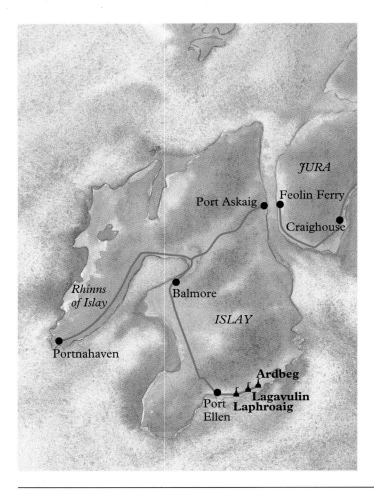

LAPHROAIG

Owner:	Allied Domecq
Age:	10 Years Old; 40%
Color:	Full gold
Aroma:	Very peaty and smoky with a tang of the sea and a hint of sweetness.
Taste:	Oily and medium-bodied, like liquid smoke. Fully peated and salty with a lingering finish.
Comment:	Essential for anyone new to malts, if only to appreciate how far the flavor spectrum extends.

LAPHROAIG®
SINGLE ISLAY MALT
SCOTCH WHISKY
AND **10** D'AGE
Years Old
The most richly flavoured of all Scotch whiskies
ESTABLISHED
1815
750mL   40%alc./vol.
PRODUIT D'ECOSSE-PRODUCT OF SCOTLAND

LAGAVULIN

Owner:	United Distillers
Age:	16 Years Old; 43%
Color:	Rich amber
Aroma:	Powerful and peaty with a pleasant burned, toasted note.
Taste:	Deep and dramatic, ranging from malt-sweet to intensely dry and heavily smoky. A touch of salt in the finish.
Comment:	A beautifully balanced malt – the Lord of the Isles.

LAGAVULIN
SINGLE ISLAY MALT WHISKY
16
SCOTCH WHISKY
43% vol   70cl e

The distillery, established in 1815, is surrounded by beds of dark, densely textured peat, though its own maltings are no longer in use. They were perhaps the last of the fully traditional maltings in the industry, relying on natural draught in the kilns and burning only peat and anthracite.

For many years Ardbeg provided the peat flavor in many Ballantine's blends, with only small amounts being bottled – 200 cases a year was not uncommon.

Its pier and huddle of buildings around the water's edge are a reminder of the days when fuel and essentials arrived at Islay's coastal distilleries by "puffers" – plucky little River Clyde cargo steamers.

Ardbeg closed in 1996, but was purchased the following year by Glenmorangie, who have plans to redevelop it as a single malt again.

Above: Lagavulin distillery sits on the edge of the shore, opposite the remains of Dunnyveg Castle, last stronghold of the Lords of the Isles.

Right: Laphroaig 10 Years Old is a challenging whisky and, with its thick flavors of peat smoke and shoreline, not for the uninitiated.

of later being a training ground for Peter Mackie, who joined the company in 1878. Mackie was a flamboyant character who went on to become one of the great names of the whisky industry and founder of White Horse blend.

Lagavulin's rich, robust persona has been prized for building the foundation of blends and helping to cement their character. Although it has one of the smokiest aromas of all the malts, it manages to combine it with grace and finesse. At 16 Years Old it is smooth, intensely flavored and made to be sipped with respect.

ARDBEG

This is the undisputed heavyweight of Scotch malt whiskies, with a body as big as a truck.

ARDBEG

Owner:	MacDonald & Muir
Age:	10 Years Old; 40%
Color:	Pale gold
Aroma:	Big, peaty and pungent with powerful notes of seaweed and peatsmoke.
Taste:	Thick and full. Like tarred rope and packed with smoke and shoreline flavors.
Comment:	Minute output for bottling, but an experience not to be missed.

The Northern Islay Malts

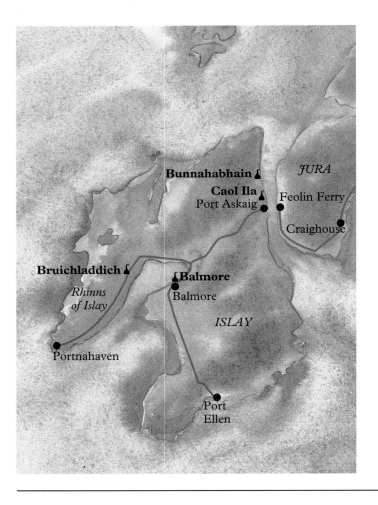

The four malts in the northern half of Islay lie on both the west and east coasts of the island. They have less attack than the southern heavyweights. The peating is more restrained, but they retain their island qualities.

BOWMORE

Bowmore is Islay's unofficial capital. The whitewashed distillery is situated in the middle of the village and plays a pivotal role in community life. The Islay and Jura Swimming Pool was converted from a bonded warehouse, with water warmed by the waste heat of Bowmore's stills.

Bowmore distillery was founded in 1779 by a local farmer who also owned the island's cargo boat. The water supply, from the Laggan River, had to be routed to the distillery across a flat plain, an engineering problem ingeniously resolved by running drops of water along waxed thread to determine the fall of the land.

Bowmore's curiously shaped pagoda chimneys dominate the high street like the towers of a Russian Orthodox church beckoning the faithful to prayer. The distillery has a modern visitors' center and produces a range of about half a dozen aged whiskies of floral elegance, which are all firmly franked with Islay character.

BRUICHLADDICH (*brew-ich-laddie*)

This is Scotland's most westerly distillery with a delicious malt considerably lighter in style than some of its Islay neighbors.

Geology, rather than geography, plays an important role in Bruichladdich's character. Along with Bowmore, which faces it across the grey waters of Loch Indaal, Bruichladdich is built on the oldest rock formations in Scotland. These two westerly distilleries draw water running over ancient grits and arkoses (quartz-bearing sandstones), which not only act as filters but also affect the type of peat developed on them.

BOWMORE

Owner:	Morrison Bowmore
Age:	12 Years Old; 40%
Color:	Amber-gold
Aroma:	Rich, dry and peaty, with touches of sea salt and lemon.
Taste:	A wide girth of flavors. Heather-honey in part. Peaty and smoky without being overpowering. A touch of dark chocolate and pears turning into a long smooth finish.
Comment:	A reliable after-dinner favorite.

BRUICHLADDICH

Owner:	Invergordon
Age:	15 Years Old; 40%
Color:	Deep straw-gold
Aroma:	Delicate and fragrant with a backbone of salty richness. Complex with a hint of banana.
Taste:	Slightly zesty with hints of spices and a nice even balance of honey, melon and citric notes.
Comment:	Deep, subtle and rewarding.

Bunnahabhain has a nice flowery quality and is popular with blenders. A soft and fairly gentle malt – the lightest of the Islay whiskies – it is an important constituent in Famous Grouse blend.

The distillery, which is the most northerly on Islay, leads a remote, tranquil existence, surrounded by its own small community. When it was built on an uninhabited part of the island, the original proprietors had to build a road, houses for its staff and a school for their children. "A civilized colony", Alfred Barnard remarked when he paid a visit. Bunnahabhain, appropriately, is an equally civilized malt whisky of balance and restraint.

CAOL ILA (*koal-eela*)

Caol Ila nestles on the Sound of Islay, south of Bunnahabhain, and is the Gaelic name for the stretch of water separating the island from Jura.

Until the 1970s, the Sound provided the distillery's link with the mainland via the celebrated little "puffer" *Pibroch*, which brought malting barley, coal and empty casks from Glasgow. Today, Caol Ila obtains its fairly heftily peated malt from Port Ellen Maltings in the south of the island.

The still room, with its six stills and floor-to-ceiling windows, commands one of the most scenic views in the industry. Outside, the sea runs treacherous currents as it sluices through the Sound, and several of Caol Ila's workers also man the Islay lifeboat, which is berthed nearby.

The distillery once housed a mission hall for the local community, where services were conducted on Sundays by a divinity student from Glasgow University.

A continuous water supply is sometimes a problem at Bruichladdich, which re-routes its supplies through cooling towers for greater efficiency in the dry summer months.

BUNNAHABHAIN (*bu-na-ha-van*)

The distillery, which was built in 1881, the same year as Bruichladdich, sits on the eastern coast of the island, gazing over the straits to Jura.

BUNNAHABHAIN

Owner:	Highland Distilleries
Age:	12 Years Old; 40%
Color:	Mid-gold
Aroma:	Fresh, delicate and quite flowery.
Taste:	The Islay that isn't an Islay: faintly peated and without pungency. Full, refreshing, fruity finish.
Comment:	An after-dinner dram with a slight hint of salt.

CAOL ILA

Owner:	United Distillers
Age:	15 Years Old; 43%
Color:	Pale gold
Aroma:	Peaty and fairly pungent with a touch of seaweed.
Taste:	Big flavored, but the smokiness is restrained, giving pleasant balance and a velvety finish.
Comment:	A middleweight Islay malt.

The Campbeltown Malts

A hundred years ago Campbeltown teemed with distilleries and was regarded as one of the most influential whisky regions in Scotland. Smoke drifting from them was as familiar as the mist drifting in from the sea.

Now, out of the thirty or so distilleries once scattered down the long finger of the Mull of Kintyre, only two remain. They stand literally at the end of the undulating highway which runs from Glasgow, three hours away, to the tip of the misty peninsula.

These days the Mull of Kintyre is more likely to evoke Paul McCartney's eponymous hit song than the memory of its robust, full-flavored whiskies. Reasons for the local industry's demise are varied: the Mull of Kintyre coalface, which provided a handy fuel source, was stripped; fashions changed, moving towards smoother styles; overproduction in a succession of whisky gluts forced distillery closures, and lastly, during the wild caprice of US Prohibition there was a discernable drop in quality of some Campbeltown whiskies. The two remaining distilleries are not accused of this, though the haste to produce in quantity for a thirsty market is said to have emasculated the region's legendary muscular character for a while.

Campbeltown may have been the birthplace of distilling in Scotland, with skills acquired from Ireland. Indeed, Bushmills distillery in Northern Ireland is possibly closer than any on Islay or the mainland.

Campbeltown whiskies are big and profound with an air of flamboyant confidence. It may be the smallest whisky region, but its malts are well received and much sought after.

Right: Campbeltown's main street. This was once the heart of a thriving single malt industry, but only two distilleries are now in business.

Campbeltown Malts – Survivors of a Great Era

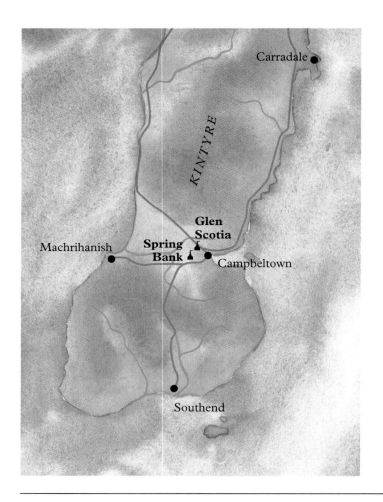

It is not uncommon, traveling through Scotland, to come across skeletal crofts and other buildings stripped of their cover standing open to the sky.

Roofs here were regularly removed to avoid incurring taxes. Such empty sepulchres can be found throughout Kintyre, the remnants of what was once a thriving whisky distilling industry.

Some buildings were converted into warehouses for the big whisky groups; others were absorbed into existing distilleries or demolished. Longrow, which did not survive to see the twentieth century, stood on the site of what has now become the car park at Springbank distillery. One of its warehouses is used as the company's bottling plant.

SPRINGBANK

The old adage about one door opening as another closes is particularly apt at Sprinkbank Distillery. It managed to survive both the Depression of the 1930s and the troubled recession of the 1980s and has now emerged as a top-selling whisky on the Japanese market.

Springbank has a long history of whisky making. The Mitchell family, who own it, once distilled illicit spirits on the same site before taking out a licence in 1828.

SPRINGBANK

Owner:	J & A Mitchell
Age:	10 Years Old; 46%
Color:	Pale straw
Aroma:	Fairly light and refreshing with a touch of sweetness.
Taste:	Creamy smooth and quite sweet with salty notes and a rounded finish.
Comment:	A highly regarded whisky – acclaimed by *The Times* tasting panel as Premier Grand Cru Classé.

Left: Springtime in Campbeltown. This is the home of Springbank distillery, where one of Scotland's most acclaimed single malts is made.

distilled a third time producing what the owners call "two and a half distillations" rather than three. The result creates a fragrant mellowness in the finished product.

The distillery is also the home of Longrow; not the original, which was once made on the site, but a malt produced in its honor – fuller and more peaty than Springbank.

GLEN SCOTIA

Glen Scotia's management has consistently believed in the importance of well-maintained casks and, accordingly, has always managed to retain a cooper on the premises.

Cask-making is something of a local speciality, rooted in a long tradition of making herring barrels, which is the same way that many of the coopers at Old Pulteney in Wick received their training.

The distillery has its own 80-foot (25m) deep wells and draws additional water from Crosshill Loch, which contributes to Glen Scotia's soft texture.

The distillery was built four years after nearby Springbank in 1832 and has been closed several times in the past century – a casualty of economic fluctuations.

In the best whisky distilling tradition, it has its own resident ghost, that of former owner Duncan MacCallum, who drowned himself in Campbeltown Loch after losing money in a business venture – an appropriate location, as it turned out. Many years later, the Scottish popular singer Andy Stewart had a minor hit with a song about someone dreaming that the loch was full of whisky.

Glen Scotia is light for a Campbeltown malt, with a character that makes its delicacy somewhat deceiving.

With the exception of Glenfiddich on Speyside, Springbank is perhaps the only "château-bottled" malt left in the industry. This is a distillery where everything, from malting to distilling, maturing and bottling, is done on the premises. Cadenhead's, the independent bottlers, are part of the company and have their malts bottled at the distillery.

Springbank's velvety smooth whisky has acquired a distinguished reputation, partly due to a curious, secretive method of almost – but not quite – triple distillation. Part of the run is

---

LONGROW

Owner:	J & A Mitchell
Age:	16 Years Old; 46%
Color:	Pale gold
Aroma:	Pungent, peaty and smoky with damp, earthy undertones.
Taste:	Dry and malty with a smooth, peaty character.
Comment:	A lovely whisky well-suited to a catholic palate.

GLEN SCOTIA

Owner:	Gibson International
Age:	8 Years Old; 40%
Color:	Mid-gold
Aroma:	Delicate and deep with a touch of peat.
Taste:	Medium-bodied and slightly peaty with a nice briny Campbeltown touch.
Comment:	An aromatic whisky of character, suitable for any occasion.

The Lowlands

Lowland malts, with their lightness of character and delicate sweetness, offer an ideal entry to the world of single malt whiskies.

As we have seen, Scotland's regional topography and weather variations strongly mould the character of malts. The changing nature of the Highlands and Islands play their part, from spicy dryness to salty ozone attributes. It naturally follows that the gentle Lowlands, extending from the border with England north to the Dumbarton–Dundee Highland line, exert their own special influence, too.

The region, which is often overlooked in favor of more characterful whiskies, has a lightness of touch that mirrors its gentle hills and burns meandering lazily between lush grassy banks. Some of the distinguished Lowland distilleries have not survived, but their memorable malts have been preserved by independent bottlers.

Among these modest classics are St. Magdalene, which closed in 1983. The distillery, built on the site of an old leper hospital, was well loved for its clean, delicate, slightly smoky whisky. Rosebank, which closed in 1993, produced a beautifully smooth, sweet, triple-distilled malt, and its demise caused a minor uproar among whisky lovers.

The Lowland survivors produce fine whiskies which are finding an expanding and appreciative audience and which are worth making the acquaintance of. Among them is Glenkinchie, a delightful, grassy whisky, which has been selected by its owners, United Distillers, to represent the Lowland style in their Classic Malt series.

Some, like Inverleven and Littlemill, go almost entirely for blending, making an important flavor contribution in contrast with the stronger Highland and Island tones.

Right: The ancient fortress of Dumbarton Castle dominates the Clyde in the heart of Lowland distilling country.

110

Soft Lowland Style

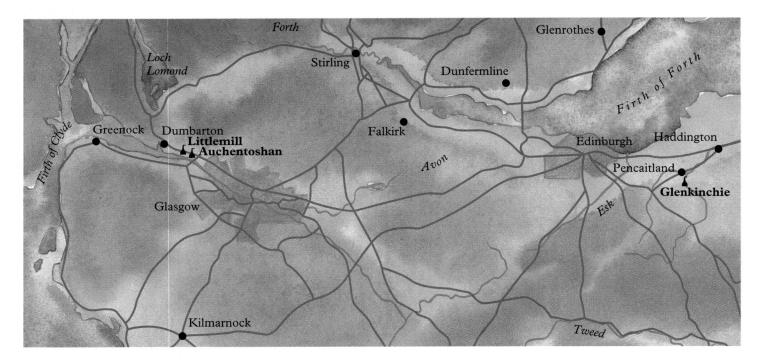

AUCHENTOSHAN (*och-an tosh-an*)

This is one of two curious distilleries (Littlemill is the other) which are located in the Lowlands, but which draw their water from a source on the other side of the Highland line. Despite sounding like a particularly explosive Scottish expletive, the Gaelic translation of its name is disappointingly humdrum; Auchentoshan simply means "the corner of the field".

The field in question lies on the edge of Glasgow overlooking the shipbuilding yards of Clydebank, which made it an unfortunate target of German wartime bombers. The dis-

AUCHENTOSHAN			GLENKINCHIE	
Owner:	Morrison Bowmore		Owner:	United Distillers
Age:	10 Years Old; 40%		Age:	10 Years Old; 40%
Color:	Light gold		Color:	Mid-amber
Aroma:	Clean and lime-fresh with a raisin sweetness and a hint of aniseed.		Aroma:	Lightly peated with a grassy fragrance.
Taste:	A well-balanced, soft-bodied whisky with a touch of fruit (tangerine?) and a sweet aftertaste.		Taste:	Restrained and slightly sweet. Pleasantly smoky for a Lowland malt.
Comment:	Smooth triple distillation makes it ideal for any occasion.		Comment:	Widely available. An excellent aperitif.

tillery, built in 1800, was heavily damaged and extensively refurbished when Morrison Bowmore purchased it in 1984.

From its vantage point, Auchentoshan has seen the rise and fall of Glasgow's shipping industry – from the departure of sailing ships loaded with legal and illegal whisky and the construction of huge liners, such as the *Queen Mary* and the *QE2*, to the vigorous trade in spices, tobacco, cotton and wine, now sadly declined.

Auchentoshan is a fragrant, light malt whisky, triple distilled for smoothness and subtlety of aroma.

GLENKINCHIE (*glen-kin-chee*)

This is one of United Distillers' six Classic Malts, chosen to represent different regional styles. The distillery is home to a museum, which is crammed with memorabilia and interesting pieces of "Heath Robinsonia". It is popular with visitors and an essential port of call for pub managers and trainee whisky executives dispatched to learn about their industry's roots.

Glenkinchie is situated in a fold of hills outside Edinburgh in an area once famous for the quality of its barley. When it opened in 1825 it traded for twelve years as Milton Distillery before changing its name – "Kinchie" is a corruption of "de Quincey", the name of the family who owned the land in the fourteenth century.

The green fields surrounding the distillery were once a "holiday camp" for city dray-horses on their annual break from hauling heavy whisky carts.

Glenkinchie is typical of the Lowland style: light and grassy with a soft texture, pleasing balance and a little sweetness. An enjoyable introduction to single malts.

LITTLEMILL

The distillery, founded in 1772, is one of the oldest in Scotland and probably the first to appoint a woman manager;

Jane Macgregor's name appeared on the first licence taken out after the 1823 Excise Act.

One of Littlemill's many curiosities is its stills – with not an inch of the usual burnished copper in sight, they are clad with aluminium insulation for heat efficiency. The idea, like most here, was the brainchild of American distiller and inventor Duncan Thomas, who bought Littlemill in 1931 and proceeded to tinker with every aspect of production in an effort to improve it. His first move was to switch from triple to double distillation to enable more scope for experimentation.

The drying kiln has twin chimneys. The stills are fitted with squat rectifying columns instead of traditional swan necks. The latter enabled Thomas to interrupt at various points in the distilling process (rather like a Coffey still) to extract spirit that aged more quickly.

This endless twiddling with production techniques meant that Littlemill, at one period, produced several different styles of malt, only one of which has survived. Years later his experiments came to fascinate Japanese distillers who shared a similar desire for change and streamlining.

Littlemill today is a soft, rounded whisky, pleasantly malty and happily unscathed by a desire for improvement.

Below: Auchentoshan, home of the only Lowland malt currently triple distilled. The extra distillation helps the whisky to mature more quickly.

LITTLEMILL

Owner:	Gibson International
Age:	8 Years Old; 43%
Color:	Pale straw
Aroma:	Delicate with touches of fruit and vanilla.
Taste:	Soft and mellow; slightly sweet and well-rounded with a smooth, dry finish.
Comment:	Not easy to come by. Good before dinner, or any time.

Single Malt Whiskies of the World

There is an hotel in Islamabad, well-known to foreign correspondents, where obtaining a dram of whisky isn't easy. To order it you have to sign an affidavit attesting that you are an alcoholic and require a drink for medical reasons. It is then brought to the privacy of your room, wrapped in a towel. By now considerable time has passed. When the swaddling is eagerly removed, the label reveals a locally distilled whiskey, which, to be kind, is a long way from Speyside.

Few countries haven't tried to make their own whiskey at one time or another. Some, like the Irish, Americans and Canadians, have evolved unique, distinctive styles. Others look to Scotland for a means of fine-tuning their national product. And then there are the strange hybrids of those who import Scotch whisky and mix it with home-distilled grain spirit.

Malt whiskies made in the Scottish manner are not so common. The Japanese have adopted the method with some success. The Irish, who possibly invented it in the first place, only have one single malt to speak of. The Welsh, who claim to have learned whisky making from the Irish, before the Scots, also have just one. Elsewhere, Scottish emigrants to far-flung corners, such as New Zealand, have attempted to replicate old techniques.

Some of these whiskies are smooth and highly acceptable, but they are clearly not Scottish single malts. Not to say that all Scotch whisky is wonderful per se. One or two, it could be argued, perhaps shouldn't have been bottled at all. Others, without being too fanciful, have contributed enormously to the quality of life and our civilized values. And, to them alone, we owe an enormous debt.

Right: Tokyo's teeming Ginza district. Single malt Scotch whisky is a status spirit here, but Japan has its own flourishing whisky industry.

Japanese Single Malts

Japanese whisky (spelled without an "e") generously acknowledges its existence as an industry to Scotch. At the turn of the century Japan had no distilleries. Now, in terms of world consumption, it is perhaps second only to the United States.

It should be said that the best Japanese single malt whiskies are excellent and, despite deriving inspiration from Scotland, have evolved an individual style of their own.

The story of the men responsible for what has become a huge industry in Japan, reads like Samurai legend. In 1918 the twenty-five-year-old heir to the Sake brewery, Masataka Taketsura, traveled to Scotland, where he spent three years learning the secrets of whisky making. He worked in Glasgow and on Speyside, but where on Speyside isn't quite certain; records show it to be Rothes, but which distillery he was employed at is no longer known.

Taketsura's epic journey is spoken of in Japan with a reverence normally reserved for monastic epic adventures and feats of endurance. In fact, Taketsura's odyssey turned out to be far from monastic: he returned with a Scottish wife, Jessie Rita, who became a highly respected pillar of Japanese society.

Back in Japan, he was taken under the wing of the wine maker, Shinjuro Torii, who was later to become the founding father of Suntory. Drawing on Taketsura's knowledge, they began distilling in 1923 and the first blended whisky, Suntory Shirofuda (now called Suntory White), was offered for sale six years later. Japan now has three major distilling companies making high-quality single malts.

Above: Barley imported from Scotland being inspected for quality before malting at Suntory's Hakushu distillery.

SUNTORY

Suntory is Japan's leading whisky producer with a market share of about 60 per cent. The company also sells around sixty well-known foreign drinks brands for forty different manufacturers.

Suntory's malt whisky is produced at three distilleries. The company malts its own barley and at any one time ages a combined total of 1,600,000 casks of whisky in cool, humid conditions not unlike those of Scotland.

Yamazaki distillery, the first to be built in Japan in 1923, has twelve pot stills. It lies in a sheltered valley outside Kyoto, known for the quality and mineral content of its local water. Torii searched Japan for some time to find a location with cool temperatures, a favorable climate and the right humidity. The resulting Yamazaki 12 Years Old Malt Whisky is medium-bodied with a rich aroma and considerable depth of flavor.

Suntory's second distillery, Hakushu, was built in 1973 at the foot of the Japanese Alps, drawing water from a stream on Kaikomagatake mountain. This is a light, estery whisky with a profound flowery, fruity aroma.

Hakushu Higashi distillery rose next door less than ten years later on the site of the original Hakushu distillery and shares it neighbor's water supply. Twelve pot stills produce a full-bodied malt with quite a soft aroma of fruit.

NIKKA

Masataka Taketsuru's ten-year contract with Suntory's founder Shinjuro Torii ended in 1934. Thus at the age of forty he found himself free to make his own whisky and promptly set up a fruit juice company to finance the operation.

Today Nikka produces two substantial single malts – Yoichi, at 10 and 12 years old, and Miyagikyo, a 12 Years Old – and enjoys a 20 per cent share of the Japanese market.

The distilleries at Hokkaido and Sendai combine Japanese grace and tranquillity with solid stone walls and elegant pagodas, reflecting Taketsuru's affection for Scottish distilling.

Hokkaido is interesting because it was founded by Taketsuru in 1934 and uses direct coal fires to heat its stills, a traditional method now rare even in Scotland. It is located on Japan's northern island, surrounded by mountains on three sides and the ocean on the other. Clean air, humidity perfect for ageing and underground springs flowing through peat produce a firm, rich, Highland-style malt whisky.

Sendai, by comparison, is a space-age operation. The "most modern distillery in the universe", as Nikka proudly puts it, where artisan skills have been almost entirely taken over by computer. The result is a soft, mild single malt comparable to the Scottish Lowland style.

SANRAKU OCEAN

Sanraku's roots lie in wine and sake, but it owns a small single malt distillery in the mountain resort of Karuizawa. Spring water comes from Mount Asama and its malt from overseas. The whisky is aromatic, fresh and slightly sweet.

Left: A portrait of Masataka Taketsuru (1894-1979), known as the father of the Japanese malt whisky industry.

Above: Suntory's medium-bodied, richly aromatic 12 Years Old malt whisky. Suntory is Japan's leading whisky producer.

117

Single Malt Whiskies of the World

Above: A waterwheel turns on the River Bush at Bushmills, Co. Antrim. St. Columb's Rill, the water source of the distillery, joins the river nearby.

IRELAND

Ireland, famous for its fragrant, silky smooth whiskies, may be the cradle of European whisky making, but it produces only one single malt.

Bushmills Malt Whiskey (the Scots claim the Irish have the "e", but they have the flavor) comes from the world's oldest distillery, licensed in 1608 in County Antrim close to the Giant's Causeway. It is aged almost entirely in bourbon casks, with little sherry influence. The American oak imparts a slight vanilla note to this extremely smooth, triple-distilled dram.

Some Scottish malts are also distilled three times – mainly Auchentoshan, Rosebank and Benrinnes, with Springbank distilled two and a half times – but Bushmills has a style and flavor quite unlike any other. It has a slightly oily body, in common with many Irish whiskies and a delicacy almost completely devoid of smoke.

The distillery's ten big pot stills produce six whiskies: four delightful malty blends and two selfs, at 5 and 10 Years Old.

ISLE OF MAN

Whiskey is spelled with an "e" here, too. Glen Kella is a "white" (i.e. colorless) single malt which has been the subject of a court action by the Scotch Whisky Association.

The island has a 100-year-old distilling tradition, but Glen Kella is something of a departure from the norm. The distillery purchases Scotch whisky and then removes its color by a secret process which was developed by Lucian Landau, a retired director of the London Rubber Company.

The method involves re-distillation and the spirit is reduced to bottling strength using local water. The result is a fragrant, peaty whisky with a rather unsettling transparent appearance, which is hard to come to terms with.

WALES

Smooth, sweetish Prince of Wales 12 Years Old Single Malt is a modern expression of a long tradition reaching back before Scottish distilling records to the fourth century when spirit of a kind was distilled by monks from Bardsey Island.

The Welsh distilling industry was quite active in the last century. Then, in the early 1900s, it was drummed out of business by the "temperance movement", which supplanted the distinctive herbal notes of its whisky (or chwisgi, as they call it) by the chapel aroma of varnish and linoleum.

Several famous names in the American bourbon industry have Welsh roots – Jack Daniel came from Cardigan and Evan Williams from Pembrokeshire.

Today's Welsh whisky began life in the 1970s by filtering imported Scotch through local herbs in the old manner and reducing the result to bottling strength with Brecon water.

NEW ZEALAND

Lammerlaw single malt hails from Dunedin, on New Zealand's South Island, where many Scots families settled in the mid-nineteenth century after the Highland clearances.

For years high taxes discouraged legal distilling. The first serious attempt to produce a home-grown product came in 1984 when Wilson's, a malt extract company, converted a brewery for whisky distilling.

The area is rich in peat and criss-crossed by streams running off the Lammerlaw Mountain. Lammerlaw Single Malt is matured for ten years in American oak to produce a full, peaty whisky in the Highland manner, with a smooth finish.

AUSTRALIA

It is still early days, but Australia's first single malt whisky is well on its way. Casks produced by a farmer of Scots descent were shipped to Springbank distillery in Campbeltown in 1996 for maturation.

It may be as long as ten years before the first Cradle Mountain Single Malt is deemed ready for drinking, but it is an inspiring start. The Tasmanian distillery, established at a cost of £150,000, uses local ingredients.

INDIA

India manufactures copious quantities of whisky of varying quality, almost all of which are blends. McDowells, who sell several million cases of blended whisky each year, claim to make India's "first and only" single malt. It is matured in bourbon barrels and is said to have a robust reputation.

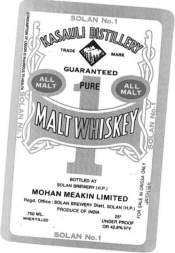

However, the claim is not quite authentic – New Delhi's Mohan Meakin brewing company produces a single malt whisky.

Distillation at Kasauli is based on traditional methods of pot distillation and floor malting. The whisky is made from pure Himalayan water which runs from natural springs down to the village. The distillery, founded in 1855 by Edward Dyer, contains maturing spirit more than 60 Years Old in its warehouses.

Rare and Unusual Whiskies

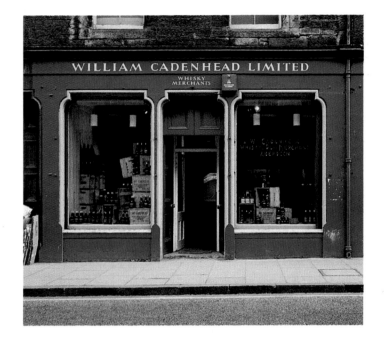

A changing industry

When Alfred Barnard completed his celebrated gazeteer of British distilleries in 1887, Scotland had 129 distilleries producing single malt whisky. Over the years that number has been eroded by recession and overproduction. During the Depression in the early 1930s it reached the gloomy low of just eight operating distilleries. However, changing fortunes in the form of record exports and the "discovery" of single malts have brought the total at the time of writing to ninety-one working distilleries.

It has been a hard procession of years for whisky. Along the way, some fine distilleries have closed their doors, never to reopen. Fortunately, their spirit lives on thanks to the enterprise and enthusiasm of independent bottlers, dedicated whisky merchants, specialist duty free shops and malt whisky societies.

For many years the vast bulk of whisky production went for blending with hardly any bottled by the distiller. In fact it was not until the 1960s that some famous brands were distillery bottled. Hitherto it had been left to grocers and bottlers to buy casks and either sell to passing custom by the jug or bottle under their label. Today a broad network of specialist shops caters for the whisky enthusiast making it easier than ever to build a collection.

Avoiding risk

There are two rules of thumb: firstly, when buying rarer whiskies, only use reputable dealers. There is good reason for this: the big merchants who bottle their own have a respected name and know what they are doing. They buy only the best casks to mature and bottle and have long experience in assessing the quality of what they are choosing. At a good shop, the staff understand their business and will be able to give the best advice tailored to whatever you need.

The second rule of thumb is resist buying whisky as an investment. Several companies advertize this service, suggesting there are profits to be made. However, allowing someone with unproven experience to purchase on your behalf may be a recipe for disaster – and your troubles won't end there. When your cask matures, the excise duty payable is likely to be a hefty amount. If you decide to sell it you will be doing so in an industry where people tend to know each other, and should you decide to keep it, you could well have difficulties finding someone who is prepared to bottle just one cask.

Rather than pick your way through this minefield, it is better by far to build your own collection at home and enjoy it at your leisure.

Where to buy

The major stockists and suppliers of rare and unusual whiskies are largely based in Britain, but deal internationally. Orders by credit card are accepted. All have mailing lists for catalogues and a few have web sites worth consulting for up-to-date details of current stock.

Gordon & MacPhail

In 1895 James Gordon and John Alexander MacPhail opened their grocers, whisky and wine merchants business in Elgin, the "whisky capital of the world". They were joined in their first year by John Urquhart, whose son and grandchildren still operate the business, which is now the world's biggest specialist whisky merchant.

Their policy has always been to select and buy new whisky, directly from distilleries, to mature it in their own bonded warehouse and bottle it when they consider it to be at its best. Because of this, some of their whiskies are extremely rare and may lie in Gordon & MacPhail's warehouse long after a distillery

Above: Gordon & MacPhail, based in Elgin on Speyside, grew from a grocer's selling whisky to the world's biggest specialist whisky merchant.

has fallen on hard times and closed.

They stock certain whiskies which were distilled in the 1960s, 1950s, 1940s and even, in very limited quantities, the 1930s – the largest selection of greatly aged whiskies in the world. Many are now extremely rare due to distillation restrictions during World War II, or because of the limited stocks. Here are some random examples from their list for anyone wishing to embark on a rare whisky collection:

1936 – Glen Grant; Mortlach
1939 – Linkwood; Old Elgin
1943 – Smith's Glenlivet
1945 – MacPhail's
1946 – Linkwood; Pride of Strathspey
1947 – MacPhail's; Old Elgin
1948 – Glen Grant; Smith's Glenlivet; Strathisla
1953 – Glen Avon
1954 – Glen Grant; Linkwood; Strathisla
1955 – Glen Avon; Longmorn; Talisker
1956 – Glen Grant
1957 – Glen Gordon; Tamdhu
1960 – Convalmore; Strathisla
1961 – Glenburgie; Glenlossie; Glenrothes; Mortlach; Old Pulteney
1964 – Ardbeg; Balblair; Tomatin
1965 – Glen Grant; Glen Mhor

Gordon & MacPhail
George House
Boroughbriggs Road
Elgin
Moray IV30 1JY
Tel: 01343 545111
Fax: 01343 540155
Website: http://www.gordonandmacphail.com

Cadenhead's

William Cadenhead founded his company in Aberdeen in 1842, but its commercial operations have long since moved to Campbeltown. Cadenhead's specialize in whisky and rum and hold the biggest stocks of old, oak-matured demerara rum in the world.

The company was a leading pioneer in the revival of interest in single malts and is famous for its bottlings of rare and old whiskies. Cadenhead's lays emphasis on the individuality of its bottlings. It is rare for more than one cask of any single whisky to be bottled at any one time. Their list therefore varies all the time and no two bottlings, even of the same age from the same distillery, are identical.

Cadenhead's has three specialist shops:

Cadenhead's Whisky Shop
172 Canongate
Edinburgh EH8 8BN
Tel: (0131) 556 5864
Fax: (0131) 556 2527

Cadenhead's Covent Garden Whisky Shop
3 Russell Street
London WC2B 5JD
Tel: (0171) 379 4640
Fax: (0171) 379 4600

Eaglesome of Campbeltown
Reform Square
Campbeltown
Argyll PA28 6JA
Tel: (01586) 551710

Milroy's

Probably the best, friendliest advice in London. Milroy's specialize in single malts and stock around 500. The shop was founded by whisky gurus and brothers John and Wallace Milroy. Wallace Milroy is the author of the best-selling *Malt Whisky Almanac*, which modestly doesn't give a single plug to this wonderful emporium.

Milroy's of Soho Ltd.
3 Greek Street
London W1V 6NX
Tel: (0171) 437 0893
Fax: (0171) 437 1345

Berry Brothers & Rudd

Established in 1698 and one of the oldest wine and whisky merchants in Britain, numbering Lord Byron, Beau Brummell, Napoleon III and the Duke of Wellington among its past customers. It was also the first merchant to open a duty free airport shop (Terminal 3, Heathrow Airport).

Berry Bros. & Rudd Ltd.
3 St James Street
London SW1A 1EG
Tel: (0171) 396 9600
Fax: (0171) 396 9619
Website: http://www.berry-bros.co.uk/

Heathrow Airport

London's Heathrow Airport has the world's finest collection of specialist tax-free whisky shops carrying an impressive range of rare and exclusive whiskies.

The Johnnie Walker Shop (Terminal 3), for example, stocked a rich, smooth, fruity blend called Honour, of which only 100 bottles were ever made.

The Glenfiddich Shop (Terminal 2) offers a 50 Years Old limited edition of 500 bottles at £3,500 each.

In Terminal 4, High Spirits sells a comprehensive range of spirits, but neighboring World of Whiskies takes some beating for its range of 160 singles and unusual blends. All the specialist shops offer free tastings with no obligation to buy. Can there a better way to wait for a flight?

The Scotch Malt Whisky Society

Formed in 1983 by a handful of devoted whisky enthusiasts with a passion for cask strength single malts, the society now has thousands of members worldwide, an informative newsletter and its own bottlings from around a hundred distilleries.

Members have access to solid, reliable experience and advice, plus members' accommodation in Leith. Worth the subscription many times over.

The Scotch Malt Whisky Society
The Vaults
87 Giles Street
Leith
Edinburgh EH6 6BZ
Tel: (0131) 554 3451
Fax: (0131) 553 1003
Website:
http://www.wdi.co.uk/smws/home.html

Adelphi Distillery

A mail order whisky company which buys and bottles unusual malts. Founded in 1993 and taking its name from a nineteenth-century Glasgow distillery pulled down in the 1960s. A reputable tasting panel and a list worth browsing.

The Adelphi Distillery Ltd.
3 Gloucester Lane
Edinburgh EH3 6ED
Tel: (0131) 226 6670
Fax: (0131) 226 6672
Website: (link)
http://www.highlandtrail.co.uk/

The Whisky Connoisseur Club

A range of single cask bottlings, blends, liqueurs and some miniatures with informative tasting notes issued every couple of months.

The Whisky Connoisseur Club
Thistle Mill
Biggar
Midlothian ML12 6LP
Tel: (01899) 221268
Fax: (01899) 220456

Blackadder International

Not a club, but a mail order company with a difference. All whiskies sold are selected by connoisseurs John Lamond and Robin Tucek, authors of the best-selling *Malt File*, who found the company in 1995.
Website: http://www.blackadder.com

See also:

The Vintage Malt Co. of Beardsen, Glasgow; Master of Malt, Tunbridge Wells, Kent. Signatory Vintage Malt Company, Leith, Edinburgh.

Distilleries that Welcome Visitors

Not all distilleries welcome visitors, particularly those that sell whisky only within the trade. Those that have properly equipped visitors centers, listed below, offer the best facilities. Smaller distilleries will often be happy to show you around if you have a genuine interest and ring the manager first to make an appointment.

Aberfeldy Distillery
Aberfeldy, Perthshire PH15 2EB
All year: November–March by appointment
Contact: distillery office (01887) 820330

Isle of Arran Distillery
Lochranza, Isle of Arran KA27 8HJ
All year: Monday–Sunday 10am–6pm;
December–February by appointment
Group bookings by appointment
Admission charge
Contact: visitor center (01290) 553255
or (01770) 830264

Ben Nevis Distillery
Lochy Bridge, Fort William PH33 6TJ
All year: Monday–Friday 9am–5pm
Easter–September: also Saturday 10am–4pm
July–August: Monday–Friday 9am–7.30pm
Group bookings by appointment
Contact: visitor center (01397) 700200

The Blair Atholl Distillery
Pitlochry, Perthshire PH16 5LY
Easter–October: Monday–Saturday 9am–5pm;
Sunday 12pm–5pm
November–Easter: Monday–Friday
9am–5pm
December–February by appointment
Group bookings by appointment
Admission charge with redemption in shop
Contact: visitor center (01796) 472234

Bowmore Distillery
Bowmore, Isle of Islay PA43 7JS
All year: Monday–Friday tours 10.30am &
2pm
Summer: also tours 11.30am & 3pm, also
Saturday tour 10.30am
Group bookings by appointment
Wheelchair access
Contact: visitor center (01496) 810441

Bunnahabhain Distillery
Port Askaig, Isle of Islay PA46 7RP
All year: Monday–Friday 10am–4pm by
appointment
Contact: distillery office (01496) 840646

Caol Ila Distillery
Port Askaig, Isle of Islay PA46 7RL
All year: Monday–Friday by appointment
Admission charge with redemption in shop
Contact: distillery office (01496) 840207

Cardhu Distillery
Knockando, Aberlour, Banffshire AB38 7RY
April–September: Monday–Saturday
9.30am–4.30pm
July–September: also Sunday 11am–4pm
December–February: Monday–Friday
10.30am–4pm
Group bookings by appointment
Admission charge with redemption in shop
Contact: visitor center (01340) 872555

Clynelish Distillery
Brora, Sutherland KW9 6LR
March–November: Monday–Friday 9.30am–
4.30pm
December–February by appointment
Group bookings by appointment
Admission charge with redemption in shop
Contact: visitor center (01408) 621033

Dalmore Distillery
Alness, Ross-shire IV17 0UT
Mid January–beginning June & mid August–
mid December: Monday–Friday
All visits by appointment
Group bookings: max 10
Contact: distillery office (01349) 882362

Dalwhinnie Distillery
Dalwhinnie, Inverness-shire PH19 1AB
January–March by appointment
March–December: Monday–Friday 9.30am–
4.30pm
June–October: also Saturday 9.30am–4.30pm
July–August: also Sunday 12.30pm–4.30pm
Group bookings by appointment
Admission charge with redemption in shop
Contact: visitor center (01528) 522208

Edradour Distillery
Pitlochry, Perthshire PH16 5JP
March–October: Monday–Saturday 9.30am–
5pm & Sunday 12pm–5pm
November–March: Monday–Saturday shop
10am–4pm
Group bookings over 14 by appointment
Contact: visitor center (01796) 472095

Fettercairn Distillery
Fettercairn, Laurencekirk, Aberdeenshire
AB30 1YB

May–September: Monday–Saturday
10am– 4.30pm
Group bookings by appointment
Contact: visitor center (01561) 340205

Glencadam Distillery
Brechin, Angus DD9 7PA
September–June: Monday–Thursday 2pm–4pm
by appointment
Group bookings: max 10
Contact: distillery office (01356) 622217

Glenfarclas Distillery
Ballindalloch, Banffshire AB37 9BD
April–September: Monday–Friday 9.30am–5pm
June–September: also Saturday 10am–4pm &
Sunday 12.30pm–4.30pm
October–March: Monday–Friday 10am–4pm.
Last tour one hour before closing time
Group bookings by appointment
Admission charge with redemption in shop
Contact: distillery office (01807) 500257

Glenfiddich Distillery
Dufftown, Banffshire AB55 4DH
Easter–Mid October: Monday–Saturday
9.20am–4.30pm & Sunday 12pm–4.30pm
Mid October–Easter: Monday–Friday
9.30am–4.30pm (Closed over Christmas &
New year)
Group bookings by appointment
Wheelchair access
Contact: visitor center (01340) 820373

Glengoyne Distillery
Dumgoyne, Nr Killearn, Stirlingshire
G63 9LB
April–November: Monday–Saturday; tours
every hour on the hour 10am–4pm; Sunday
12pm–4pm
April–October: Nosing session Wednesdays
7.30pm booking essential
Group bookings by appointment
Admission charge
Contact: visitor center (01360) 550254

Glen Grant Distillery
Rothes, Aberlour, Morayshire IV33 7BS
Mid March–end May: Monday–Saturday
10am–4pm & Sunday 11.30am–4pm
June–September: Monday–Saturday
10am–5pm
Admission charge with redemption in shop
includes visit to Victorian Gardens
Group bookings by appointment
Wheelchair access
Contact: visitor center (01542) 783318

Glenkinchie Distillery
Pencaitland, East Lothian EH34 5ET
All year: Monday–Friday 9.30am–4.30pm
March–October: also Saturday & Sunday
12pm–4pm
Group bookings by appointment
Admission charge with redemption in shop
Contact: visitor center (01875) 340451

The Glenlivet Distillery
Ballindalloch, Banffshire AB37 9DB
Mid March–end October: Monday–Saturday
10am–4pm & Sunday 12.30pm–4pm
July & August: remains open until 6pm daily
Group bookings by appointment
Wheelchair access
Contact: visitor center (01542) 783220

Glenmorangie Distillery
Tain, Ross-shire IV19 1PZ
All year: Monday–Friday 10am–4pm
June–October: also Saturday 10am–4pm
Regular tours from 10.30am
Advance booking advisable
Admission charge
Contact: visitor center (01862) 892477

Glen Ord Distillery
Muir of Ord, Ross-shire IV6 7UJ
All year: Monday–Friday 9.30am–5pm
December–February by appointment
Group bookings by appointment
Admission charge with redemption in shop
Contact: visitor center (01463) 872004

Glenturret Distillery
The Hosh, Crieff, Perthshire PH74HA
January: Monday–Friday 11.30am–4.30pm
February: also Saturday & Sunday
11.30am–4.30pm
March–December: Monday–Saturday
9.30am–6pm & Sunday 12pm–6pm
Group bookings by appointment
Admission charge
Contact: distillery office (01764) 656565

Highland Park Distillery
Holm Road, Kirkwall, Orkney KW15 1SU
January–February by appointment
April–October: Monday–Friday 10am–5pm
July–August: also Saturday & Sunday
12pm–5pm
November, December, March: Monday–
Friday tour at 2pm & 3.30pm
Group bookings by appointment
Admission charge with redemption in shop
Contact: visitor center (01856) 875632

Isle of Jura Distillery
Craighouse, Isle of Jura PA60 7XT
September–May: Monday–Friday 9am–4pm
by appointment
Contact: distillery office (01496) 820240

Knockando Distillery
Knockando, Aberlour, Banffshire AB38 7RP
All year: Monday–Friday 10am–4pm
by appointment
Contact: distillery office (01340) 810205

Lagavulin Distillery
Port Ellen, Isle of Islay PA42 7DZ
All year: Monday–Friday 9am–4.30pm
All visits by appointment
Admission charge with redemption in shop
Contact: distillery office (01496) 302250

Laphroaig Distillery
Port Ellen, Isle of Islay PA42 7DU
September–June: Monday–Thursday tours
10.30am & 2.30pm by appointment
Contact: distillery office (01496) 302418

Macallan Distillery
Craigellachie, Banffshire AB38 9RX
All year: Monday–Friday: tours 10am, 11am,
12pm, 2pm, 3pm & 4pm by appointment
Contact: distillery office (01340) 871471

Miltonduff-Glenlivet Distillery
Elgin, Morayshire IV30 3TQ
September–June: Monday–Thursday 10am–
2pm by appointment
Contact: distillery office (01343) 554121

Oban Distillery
Oban, Argyllshire PA34 5NH
All year: Monday–Friday 9.30am–5pm
Easter–October: also Saturday 9.30am–5pm
December–February by appointment
Group bookings by appointment
Admission charge with redemption in shop
Contact: visitor center (01631) 572004

Royal Locknagar Distillery
Craithie, Ballater, Aberdeenshire AB35 5TB
All year: Monday–Friday 10am–5pm
Easter–October: also Saturday 10am–5pm &
Sunday 11am–4pm
Group bookings by appointment
Admission charge with redemption in shop
Contact: distillery office (01339) 742273

Strathisla Distillery
Keith, Banffshire AB55 3Bs
February–mid March: Monday–Friday
9.30am–4pm
Mid March–end November: also Saturday
9.30am–4pm & Sunday 12.30pm–4pm
Group bookings by appointment
Admission charge with redemption in shop
Contact: visitor center (01542) 783044

Talisker Distillery
Carbost, Isle of Skye IV47 8SR
April–June: Monday–Friday 9am–4.30pm
July–August: also Saturday 9am–4.30pm

December–February: Monday–Friday
1.30pm–5pm
Group bookings by appointment
No coaches
Admission charge with redemption in shop
Contact: visitor center (01778) 640314

Tamnavulin Distillery
Ballindalloch, Banffshire AB37 9JA
Easter–October: Monday–Friday 10am–4pm
Group booking by appointment
Contact: visitor center (01807) 590 442

Tobermory Distillery
Tobermory, Isle of Mull PA75 6NR
Easter–October: Monday–Friday 10am–5pm
October–Easter by appointment
Group bookings by appointment
Admission charge with redemption in shop
Contact: distillery office (01688) 302645

Tomatin Distillery
Tomatin, Inverness-shire IV13 7YT
All year: Monday–Friday 9am–4.30pm
May–October: also Saturday 9am–1pm
Group bookings by appointment
Wheelchair access
Contact: visitor center (01808) 511444

Tomintoul Distillery
Ballindalloch, Banffshire AB37 9AQ
Mid January–beginning June & mid August–
mid December: Monday–Friday
All visits by appointment
Group bookings: max 10
Contact: distillery office (01807) 590274

The Tormore Distillery
Advie, Grantown-on-Spey, Morayshire
PH26 3LR
September–June: Monday–Thursday
1.30pm–4pm by appointment
Group bookings: max 8
Contact: head office (01389) 765111

The Malt Whisky Trail
If you visit Speyside, the heartland of single
malt whisky production, call at any tourist
office for details of the signposted,
seventy-mile (113km) trail of eight of the
greatest distilleries: Cardhu, Glenfarclas,
Glenfiddich, Glen Grant, The Glenlivet,
Strathisla, Tamdhu and Tamnavulin. But
remember, if you are tasting, get someone to
do the driving for you.

Index

Bibliography

Andrews, Allen *The Whisky Barons*, Jupiter 1977
Barnard, Alfred *The Whisky Distilleries of the United Kingdom*, Lochar 1987
Brown, Gordon *The Whisky Trails*, Prion 1993
— *Classic Spirits of the World*, Prion 1995
Coffey, Thomas M. *The Long Thirst*, Hamish Hamilton 1976
Dickens, Cedric *Drinking with Dickens*, private printing 1980
Gunn, Neil M. *Whisky & Scotland*, Souvenir 1977
Hills, Philip (ed.) *Scots on Scotch*, Mainstream 1991
Jackson, Michael *The World Guide to Whisky*, Dorling Kindersley 1987
— *Michael Jackson's Malt Whisky Companion*, Dorling Kindersley 1989
Lamond, John & Tucek, Robin *The Malt File*, Benedict Books 1989
Lee, Henry *How Dry We Were*, Prentice-Hall 1963
Lockhart, Sir Robert Bruce *Scotch*, Putnam 1951
Maclean, Charles *The Mitchell Beazley Pocket Whisky Book*, Mitchell Beazley 1993
— *Discovering Scotch Whisky*, NewLifeStyle 1996
Milroy, Wallace *Malt Whisky Almanac*, Lochar 1986
Morrice, Philip *Schweppes Guide to Scotch*, Alphabooks 1983
Moss, Michael & Hulme, John *The Making of Scotch Whisky*, James & James 1981
Nown, Graham *The English Godfather*, Ward Lock 1987
Regan, Gary & Mardee Haidin *The Book of Bourbon*, Chapters 1996
Sillett, Steve *Illicit Scotch*, Beaver Books 1965
Townsend, Brian *Scotch Missed*, Neil Wilson 1993
Wilson, Ross *Scotch Made Easy*, Hutchinson 1959

Acknowledgments

Grateful thanks for help and valuable assistance to Ballantines, for permission to quote from the author's history of Ballantines 17 Years Old, The Scotch; and especially Ken Lindsay of Allied Domecq; Iain Henderson, Laphroaig; Margaret McIntosh of The Keepers of the Quaich; Jim McEwan and Glen Moore, Morrison Bowmore; Tony Tucker and Caroline Thomson-Glover, The Scotch Whisky Association; Ian Urquart and Leslie Duroe, Gordon & MacPhail; Euan Mitchell, Springbank Distillers; Cheryl Campsie, Richard Mulcaster Associates; Alan Murray and Mairi Sih, Cadenhead's; Patrick Millet, J & B; Malcolm Greenwood, J & G Grant.

Picture Credits